WOOD WORKS

WOOD WORKS

EXPERIMENTS
WITH COMMON WOOD AND TOOLS

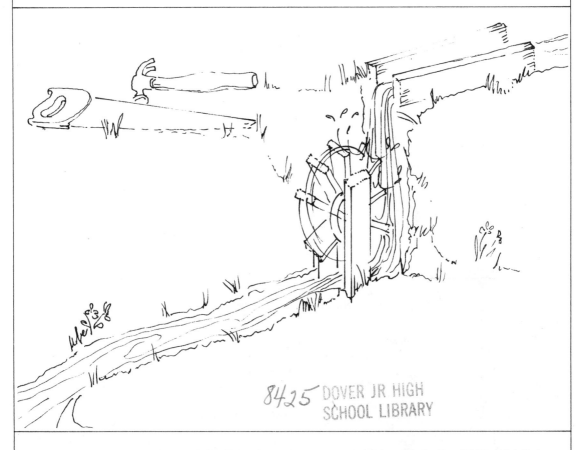

by WILLIAM F. BROWN illustrated by M.G. BROWN

ATHENEUM **1984** NEW YORK

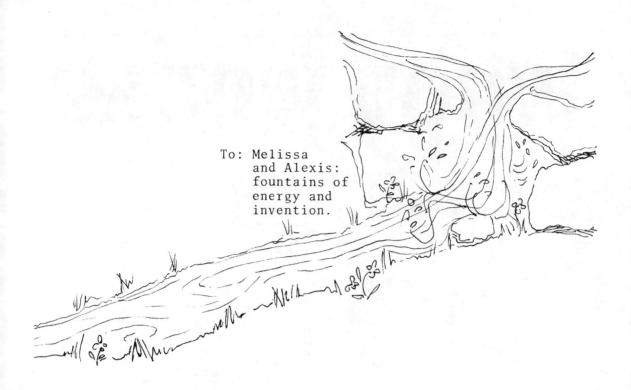

To: Melissa
and Alexis:
fountains of
energy and
invention.

The map on page 48 and the Dymaxion tent are based
on concepts of Buckminster Fuller.

LIBRARY OF CONGRESS CATALOGING IN PUBLICATION DATA

Brown, William F.   Wood Works.

SUMMARY: Detailed instructions for making a variety
of toys, structures, and objects from wood.
1. Woodwork—Juvenile literature.   [1. Woodwork]
I. Brown, Mary Geiger, 1943–   . II. Title.
TT185.B78   1984   684'.08   83-15905
ISBN 0-689-31033-1

CONTENTS

TOOLS   MATERIALS

PROJECTS

APPENDIX

NOTES FOR PARENTS AND TEACHERS

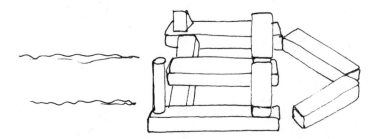

Children have a natural urge to build. It's their way of discovering how the world works; it's their way of learning they can shape the world around them. Yet many children end their active building with the block play of their kindergarten years. In our research for this book, we asked: what frustrates this essential creative activity? We found a paradox: the growth of sophisticated technology in our everyday lives exiles the simple technology of wood and hand tools. Materials and tools that a child can use are not always available, as they once were. Reference models, things in the child's world that a child can copy in simple building, have become obscure. This paradox is significant because the natural foundation for understanding advanced technology is the physical and intellectual learning of the child's experiments with tools and building.

We designed this book to give children access to tools. We outline the plan for you here because there are obstacles with which a child needs help.

TOOLS
We designed the work for two basic tools, the hammer and saw, complemented by safety goggles, a clamp, a square, and a measurer. We worked around tools that are more difficult to master or obtain, most notably the drill. The inexpensive electric drill has made adequate and affordable hand drills difficult to get. Some of the circumventions are a little awkward, adding masts to sail boats, for example. But we wanted a set of tools every child has access to. The Buying Guide in Appendix 2 suggests a complete set for under twenty dollars.

BENCH
A child needs a place to work. We found that a small bench is better. Appendix 4 suggests designs that, though beyond a child's ability to build, an adult can assemble in an hour.

MATERIALS
We've encouraged finding wood, but some wood will have to be bought. So we developed the designs around 1x3 furring, the least expensive wood available anywhere. All but two of the projects require less than a dollar's worth of materials each.

HELP

We've encouraged children to ask for help. They'll need help assembling the tools and materials, help interpreting some of the instructions, and help occasionally with frustrating steps. Children have traditionally learned woodworking from watching and working with others, not from books. You don't need woodworking skills to help. We've tried to design the book so that your common sense and patience are the only master skills your apprentice will need.

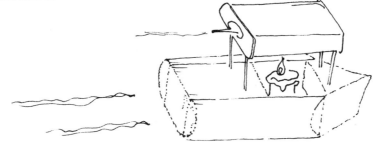

SAWING

Sawing is the most difficult work in the book. The projects are worked out with tolerances for the wanderings of a beginning sawer. The beginning sawer will still need encouragement. If you have a power saw or a friend with a power saw, you might cut the few plywood pieces the projects require. Long cuts in plywood are difficult even for experienced hand sawers.

PROJECTS

We've chosen for the projects things that work, adapted from historic technology. There are two reasons:

Function is more important than form. Finished beauty is difficult for a child's skill and materials. Precision and finished beauty develop with time. These projects have a more immediate test of success: if it works, it's right.

Sailboats and water wheels are the technology of energy that a child can see and touch. Our children live in a world of invisible wonders, a world of microchips and electron streams. It is unfortunately a world that a child cannot take apart to see how it works. We turned to projects a child can explore with all the senses. We drew from the history of invention projects that are the building blocks of modern technology.

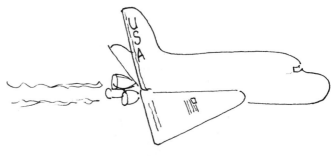

WOOD WORKS

INTRODUCTORY PUZZLE--IT ALL FITS TOGETHER

Getting started is the hardest part of building.
You need a place to work.
You need tools.
You need materials.
It's like making a puzzle: you have to find the pieces.

We designed the projects in this book to help.
You need only 7 basic tools:

    a hammer, a saw and safety goggles,
    a clamp and a bench,
    a measurer and a square.

You need only materials that are inexpensive
or that you can find in your neighborhood.
If we weren't sure you could find what
you need for a project,
we scrapped it.

Getting started still takes time and your own plan.
A good place to start is with
the one--sometimes forgotten--piece
of the puzzle that can help you
organize all the other pieces.

A HELPER

friend   mother   father   little   grand-   neighbor
                               sister   father

Do it yourself does not mean do it alone. Learn to use
help: it's an important tool.

Sawing long cuts, putting projects together, or just
figuring out instructions--you'll get stuck. Don't be
shy, find help. You may not need an expert, or even a
grown-up, but two heads instead of one, three hands
instead of two.

                    What do I need?
    Ask yourself   Who can help?

Too much help isn't helpful. You don't need
someone to take over your project. Say what
you need...and what you don't need. You'll
help your helper.

Buddy Plan: a nice way to use this book,
           or, one plus one equals more
           than two.

Invite a friend over.
Work on the same project.
    Take turns doing the steps, watch each other.
    You'll help each other and teach each other.
    Two working together do more than either
    working alone.

Sometimes you'll need advice. . .

Getting started,

'Where can I find a spool?'
'Can I use this board?'

Instructions,

'What does this mean?'

Uncertainty,

'Does this look right?'
'Do you think I need help?'

Often you'll discover answers in just saying aloud your questions.

Sometimes you'll need a hand. . .

Holding

No tool is as clever as an extra hand.

Steadying

A hand alongside yours will teach
yours smooth strokes.

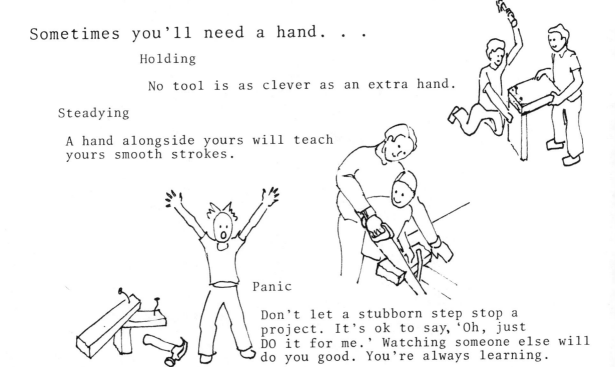

Panic

Don't let a stubborn step stop a
project. It's ok to say, 'Oh, just
DO it for me.' Watching someone else will
do you good. You're always learning.

HAMMER

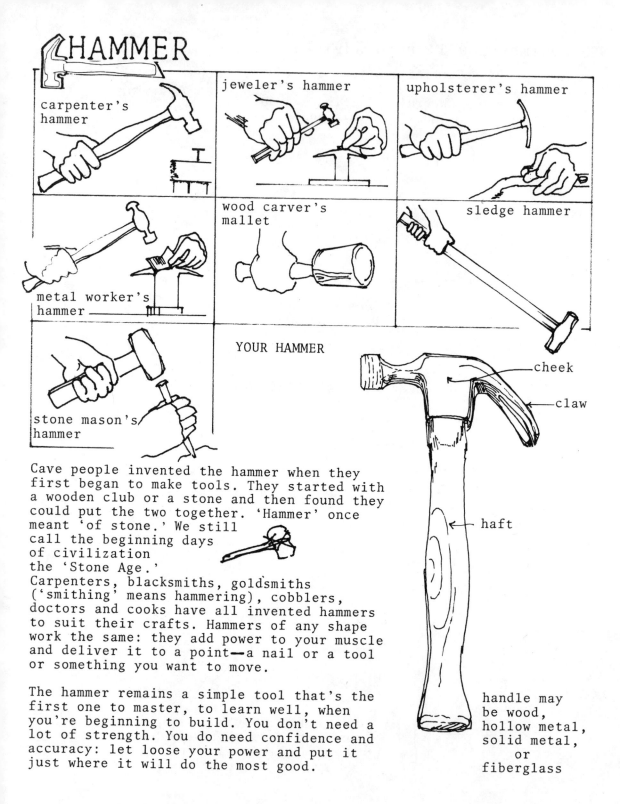

carpenter's hammer

jeweler's hammer

upholsterer's hammer

metal worker's hammer

wood carver's mallet

sledge hammer

stone mason's hammer

YOUR HAMMER

cheek

claw

haft

handle may be wood, hollow metal, solid metal, or fiberglass

Cave people invented the hammer when they first began to make tools. They started with a wooden club or a stone and then found they could put the two together. 'Hammer' once meant 'of stone.' We still call the beginning days of civilization the 'Stone Age.'
Carpenters, blacksmiths, goldsmiths ('smithing' means hammering), cobblers, doctors and cooks have all invented hammers to suit their crafts. Hammers of any shape work the same: they add power to your muscle and deliver it to a point—a nail or a tool or something you want to move.

The hammer remains a simple tool that's the first one to master, to learn well, when you're beginning to build. You don't need a lot of strength. You do need confidence and accuracy: let loose your power and put it just where it will do the most good.

TWO HINTS: SWINGING. . .

At first it may seem that you just grab the hammer and swing. As you practice you will learn that the swing comes from three parts of your arm. To understand this, imagine that your arm is part of the hammer. Imagine that you have a robot arm. There would be three joints.

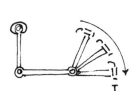

the wrist

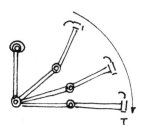

the elbow

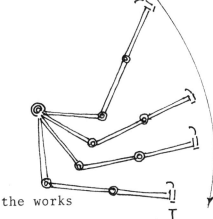

the works

When you swing mostly from the wrist, your aim is good, your power very little.

Swinging from the elbow with the wrist nearly stiff gives you much more power. It keeps a smooth stroke.

To drive big nails, you must work from your shoulder. Now all of your muscles join in. The hammer head moves fast: speed moves nails.

Your arm is much more complicated than this machine. But your brain might remind it, from time to time, that the wrist should not be asked to do all the work. Once you learn to swing from your elbow, the rest of your arm will learn to follow.

————————REMIND YOUR ELBOW TO WORK ALONG WITH YOUR WRIST!————

. . .AND HOLDING YOUR HAMMER

At first, everyone wants to hold the hammer very close to the head. You are sure to hit the nail that way. But you really won't hit it very hard. And you may find yourself pushing nails over, not in.

The hammer is made to be held near its end. When you hold it at its end, it will give its most powerful and straight push.

————————REMIND YOUR HAND TO MOVE BACK!————

HAMMER SKILLS

hammering

Most often you use your hammer to put boards together.

starting nails

Nail is held between thumb and first finger. Tap it well into the wood before you strike it hard.

Small nails are pushed through cardboard or stiff paper to be held for starting. (So fingers are clear of the hammer.) Then pull the cardboard off before finishing the nail.

splitting headaches: preventive medicine

1. Hold down well. Work on a solid table or floor. Bounce is bad.

2. Avoid nailing in lines along the grain.

3. Don't try to nail through knots.

4. Always nail from the thinner to the thicker piece of wood.

5. If all else fails see the section on glue.

with tools

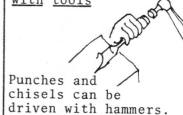

Punches and chisels can be driven with hammers.

straightening

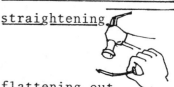

flattening out old, bent nails. .

clinching

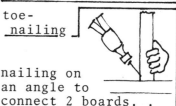

Bending over nails that have come through makes a strong connection.

toe-nailing

nailing on an angle to connect 2 boards. .

pulling

The hammer claw pulls nails. It's a second tool that was built into the hammer fairly recently.

Be careful with difficult nails. The hammer becomes a powerful lever: handles break.

A block beneath the hammer will give you a smoother pull.

The claw can also straighten a bent nail.

Some nails just won't let go. Work around the stubborn nail, or borrow a crowbar.

SAFETY GOGGLES. . .

Carpenters' hands expect splinters and an occasional banged thumb.
Hands heal easily. Eyes don't.

A hammer strikes a nail with hundreds of pounds of force.
Sometimes the force strikes back. The board shatters. A
nail flies up. Goggles prevent injuries. Make it a habit
to wear goggles when you work.

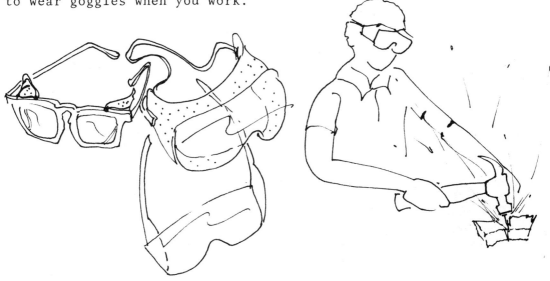

Goggles come in many styles. Simple glasses style, eye shields,
give good protection. Select goggles that are comfortable for
you to wear. Drugstores and opticians sell straps that will
improve the fit and comfort of inexpensive eye shields.

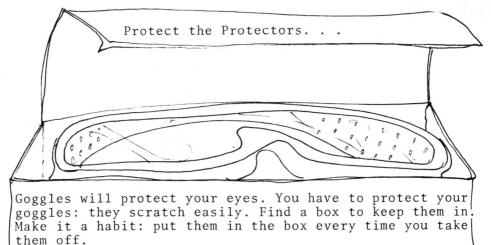

Protect the Protectors. . .

Goggles will protect your eyes. You have to protect your
goggles: they scratch easily. Find a box to keep them in.
Make it a habit: put them in the box every time you take
them off.

9

. . .AND COMMON SENSE

You don't need a long list of *do's* and *don't's*.
Listen to your common sense and pay attention. You'll learn
how to handle your tools carefully.

There are a few lessons you shouldn't learn the hard way:

Hair. . .

If you have long hair, tie it up or
wear a cap. The claw of a hammer will
catch long hair and give it a painful
jerk.

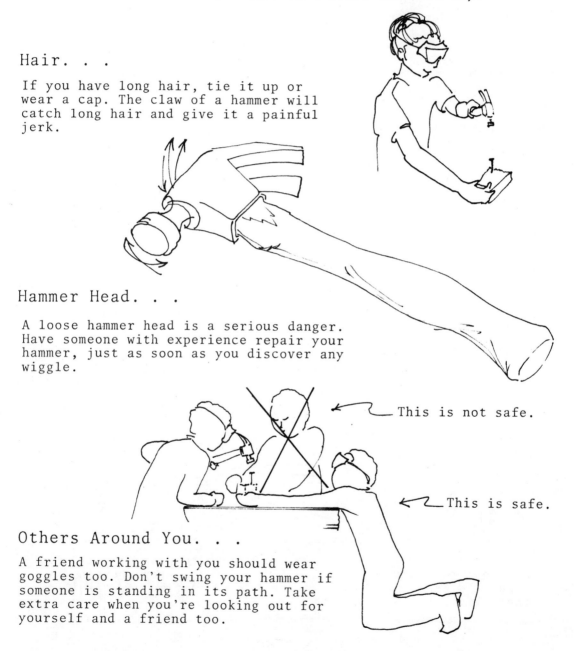

Hammer Head. . .

A loose hammer head is a serious danger.
Have someone with experience repair your
hammer, just as soon as you discover any
wiggle.

This is not safe.

This is safe.

Others Around You. . .

A friend working with you should wear
goggles too. Don't swing your hammer if
someone is standing in its path. Take
extra care when you're looking out for
yourself and a friend too.

SAW

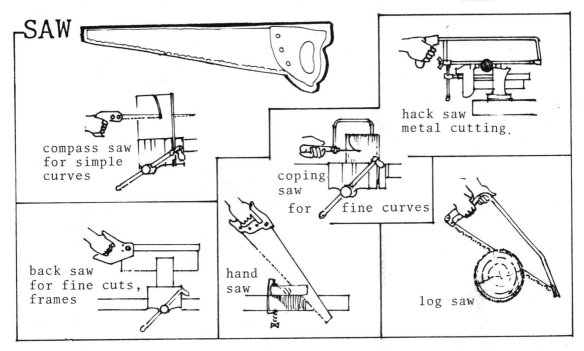

compass saw
for simple
curves

hack saw
metal cutting.

coping
saw
for fine curves

back saw
for fine cuts,
frames

hand
saw

log saw

Saws are made to tear through the trunks of great trees, to cut cooly through iron...and to trim the turns of a violin face. All saws are delicate tools that do difficult jobs. Their blades must be straight, their teeth sharp, their owners respectful.

Saws are shaped for their work. The thin blade of a coping saw cuts curves, the wide blade of a back saw makes fine, straight cuts. The large teeth of a log saw cut fast, the finer teeth of a hack saw cut slowly.

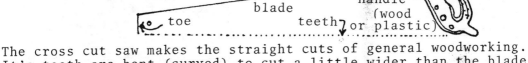

blade   handle
toe   teeth (wood
or plastic)

The cross cut saw makes the straight cuts of general woodworking. It's teeth are bent (curved) to cut a little wider than the blade itself. The blade travels through the span of this cut: its *kerf*.

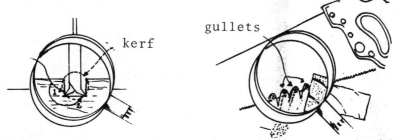

kerf

gullets

The space between the teeth, the *gullets*, carry away the bits of wood cut by the teeth. That's sawdust.

SAWING SKILLS

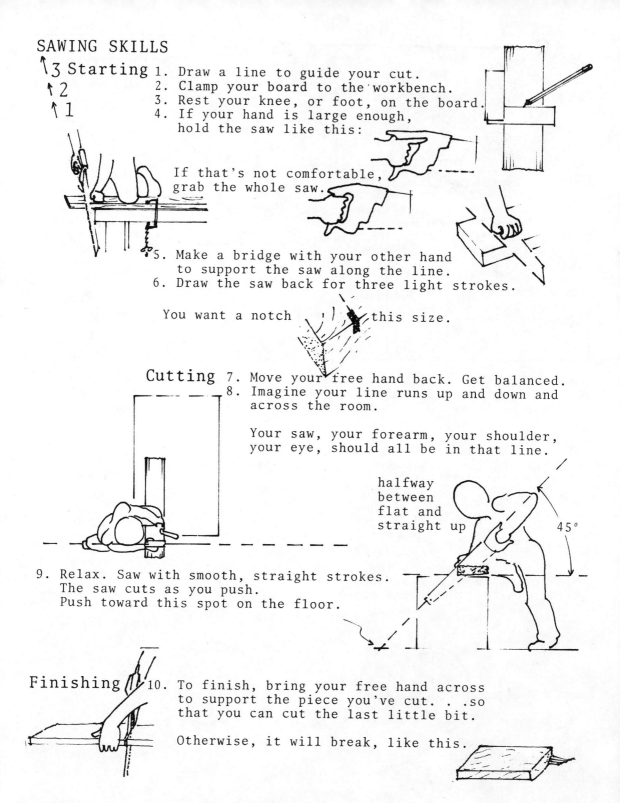

↑3 Starting
↑2
↑1

1. Draw a line to guide your cut.
2. Clamp your board to the workbench.
3. Rest your knee, or foot, on the board.
4. If your hand is large enough, hold the saw like this:

If that's not comfortable, grab the whole saw.

5. Make a bridge with your other hand to support the saw along the line.
6. Draw the saw back for three light strokes.

You want a notch this size.

Cutting

7. Move your free hand back. Get balanced.
8. Imagine your line runs up and down and across the room.

Your saw, your forearm, your shoulder, your eye, should all be in that line.

halfway
between
flat and
straight up

45°

9. Relax. Saw with smooth, straight strokes. The saw cuts as you push. Push toward this spot on the floor.

Finishing

10. To finish, bring your free hand across to support the piece you've cut. . .so that you can cut the last little bit.

Otherwise, it will break, like this.

12

TYPES OF SAWING

Cross Cutting

These are the steps for crosscutting: the sawing you'll do most.

Wood is a bundle of fibers. Imagine a hand full of grass. It's easiest to cut across the fibers. Your saw is made for this type of cutting.

Other cutting requires changes in the steps:

Rip Cutting

Cutting along the grain is called *ripping*. Imagine cutting into the handful of grass. Fibers get twisted: it's harder to keep a straight line.

1. Clamp the wood upright.
2. Start on the edge near you.
3. Saw almost straight across.
4. Guide the saw with your free hand.

Plywood Cutting

In plywood, the grain goes *both* directions.

1. Cut as for cross cutting.
2. But keep your saw at a very low angle.

Long cuts in plywood with a handsaw are difficult. If you need to cut a lot of plywood, find a friend with a power saw.

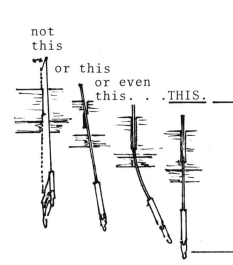

not this
or this
or even
this. . .THIS.

15°

The secret to sawing is keeping the saw straight...in the groove. These steps help; the hints on the next two pages help, then it takes practice. LOTS of practice.

HINTS. . . .Preparing for cuts saves time in cutting.
Vibrations
You can't saw a moving line.

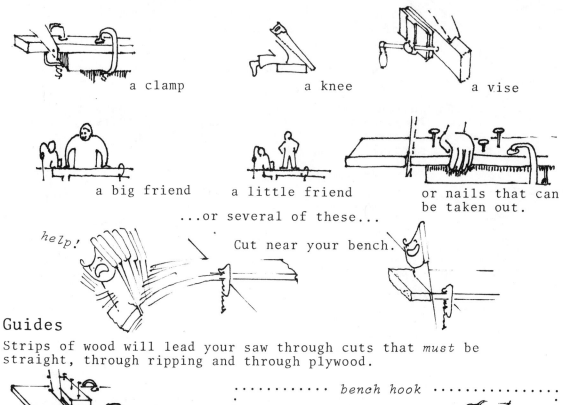

a clamp   a knee   a vise

a big friend   a little friend   or nails that can be taken out.

...or several of these...

help!

Cut near your bench.

Guides
Strips of wood will lead your saw through cuts that *must* be straight, through ripping and through plywood.

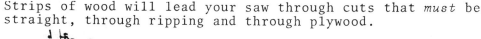

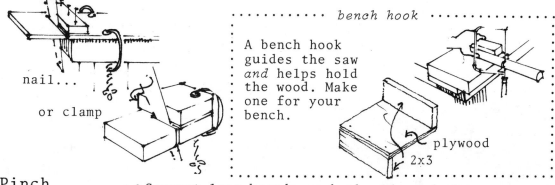

nail...

or clamp

.... *bench hook* ....

A bench hook guides the saw *and* helps hold the wood. Make one for your bench.

plywood
2x3

Pinch
Support long boards on both sides of the cut.

ouch!

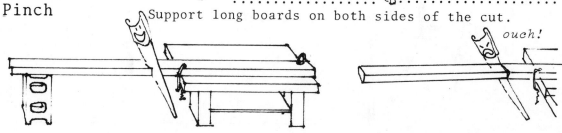

If you've practiced
  and still find sawing difficult:

Take a second look at your saw:

Is it sharp?
Many old saws and some new ones aren't.
Running into one nail can dull a saw.

Is it straight?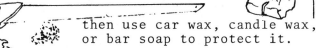
A crooked saw will bind or trip.

Is it clean?
Clean off rust, paint or pitch, and
then use car wax, candle wax,
or bar soap to protect it.

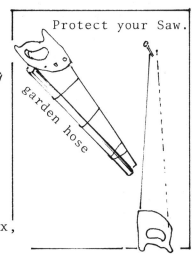

Protect your Saw.

garden hose

If you're not sure about your saw, have an experienced builder
cut with it. He or she will know if it's not cutting the way a
saw is supposed to.

Take a second look at your wood:

Is it cut-able?
Avoid hardwood,
        knots,
          particle board,

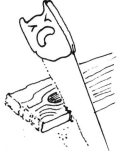

and wet wood.

Different Strokes. . .

両
双

RYOBA

FRAME SAW

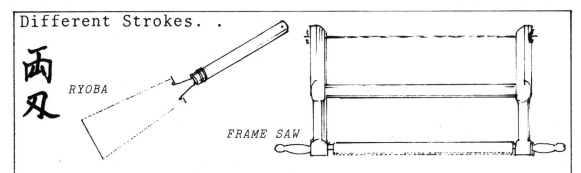

In Japan, children learn to saw with a *RYOBA*, which cuts on
the pull instead of the push.

In Europe, some children learn with a *FRAME SAW*, which is held
with two hands and cuts on the push and the pull.

15

CLAMPS

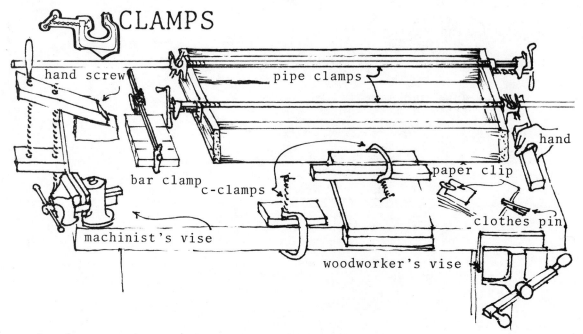

hand screw

pipe clamps

hand

bar clamp

c-clamps

paper clip

clothes pin

machinist's vise

woodworker's vise

Woodworkers need more than two hands. For cutting, gluing and assembling, two hands are just not enough.

Abracadabra..............
a magic helper: the clamp.

This third hand grips 200 times harder than your own built-in versatile clamps.

Trust its magic. It's a tool as important as your hammer or saw. Like those tools, it takes practice to use. Working a clamp is simple. 'Using' a clamp means finding the positions and tricks to simplify your work. Woodworkers have invented clamps in a hundred shapes and sizes. With imagination, you can invent a hundred uses for a simple c-clamp.

A clamp can . . .

make sawing easier

wood scrap
prevents marking

hold work for testing

frame:
malleable iron,
aluminum, or
pressed steel

steady work for nailing

shoe

screw

pinch work while glue dries

pull stubborn boards together

hold a board while you pull nails . . .

Just one caution:

sliding tommy bar

Keep your clamp clear of
your saw's path.

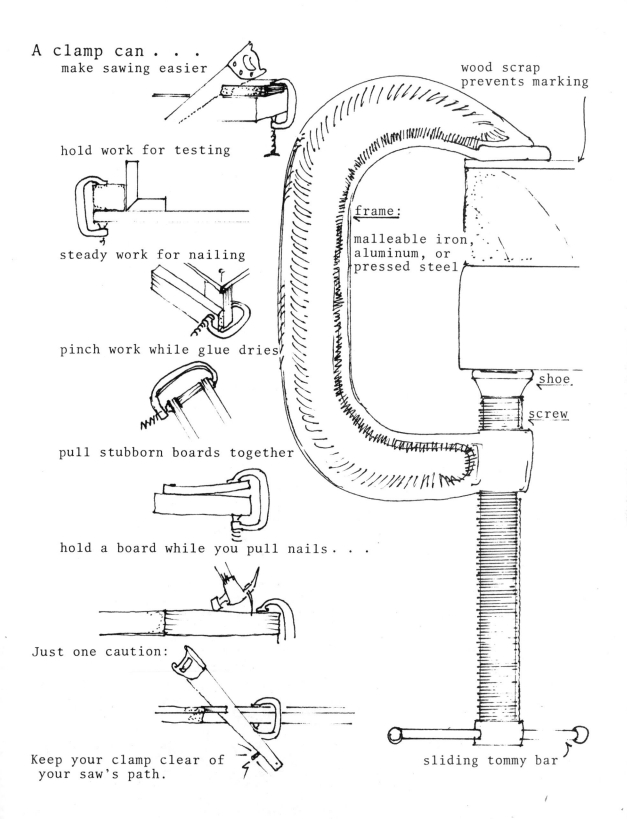

WORKBENCH

A workbench is a tool. Like other tools it has its own jobs to perform.

It must hold your work at the right height. (The saw is very fussy about this.)

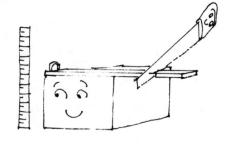

It must allow you to hold your work with clamps, both flat and up and down.

It must be steady. It must not shake or slide while you work.

It must be kind to your tools. No nails or metal parts should catch the saw.

It might have to store your tools or wood scraps.

It might have to be moveable so it can be stored when you're not working.

Because a bench must do so many jobs, no one bench is best for everyone. A bench does not have to be fancy or expensive. Study the ideas shown here. Talk it over with your mother or father. See what's available. Then decide which bench will do the best job for you.

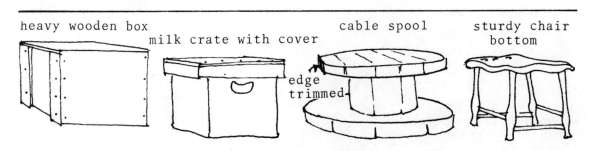

heavy wooden box

milk crate with cover

cable spool

edge trimmed

sturdy chair bottom

How big should a bench be?

The top (working surface) of a bench can be any size. A small bench top is fine.

With any size bench, you'll have to find ways to work with projects bigger than the bench, sometimes.

How tall?

This is a more difficult question.

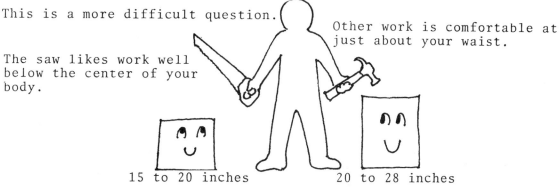

The saw likes work well below the center of your body.

Other work is comfortable at just about your waist.

15 to 20 inches   20 to 28 inches

You will be wise to look for a low bench. It's easier to hammer on a low bench than to saw on a high one. Low benches are also easiest to make and store. The height is right for comfortable work kneeling. . .a posture fine carpenters in Japan prefer.

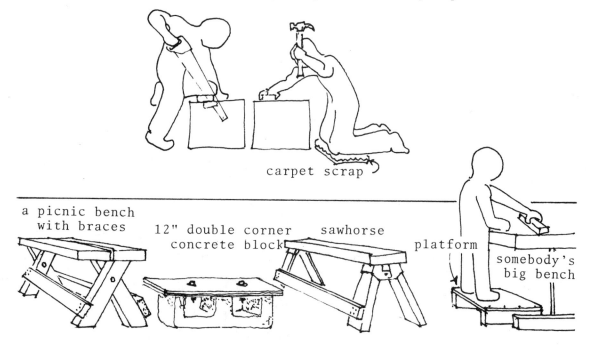

carpet scrap

a picnic bench with braces

12" double corner concrete block

sawhorse

platform

somebody's big bench

How steady?
Very steady.

You have to find ways to hold work steady for sawing *and* hammering.
Work shouldn't wiggle, vibrate or slide.

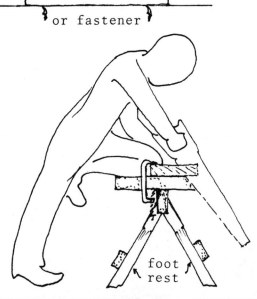

Clamps help, friends help. But beneath
it all, you need a bench that will help.

First the top must be solid, no v*ibrtaoin*. A well-supported,
tightly fastened top will take care of this.

Then you have a choice:

    If your bench has a permanent home,
    attach it to wall or floor, or make
    it heavy. Add a sand bag, a cement
    block or bricks for extra weight.

weight

or fastener

or

If you want a moveable bench,
learn to use *your* weight to make
it steady. With a little practice,
you'll find a posture that is
balanced and comfortable.

foot
rest

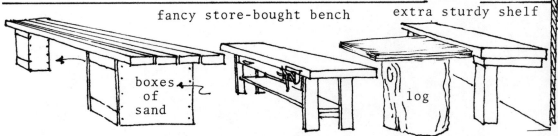

fancy store-bought bench   extra sturdy shelf

boxes
of
sand

log

MEASURER

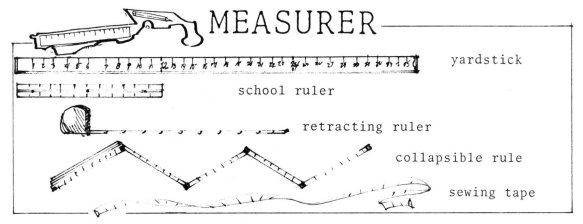

yardstick

school ruler

retracting ruler

collapsible rule

sewing tape

You have used a ruler in school. Builders use many styles of measurers. These fold and unfold, or slide, or wind up. They may be wood metal, cloth or plastic. They all measure the same as a simple school ruler.

Measuring for building is more than reading numbers. It's learning to use those numbers cleverly and simply. As you build the projects in this book, you'll develop a 'feel' for numbers and sizes. Here's how.

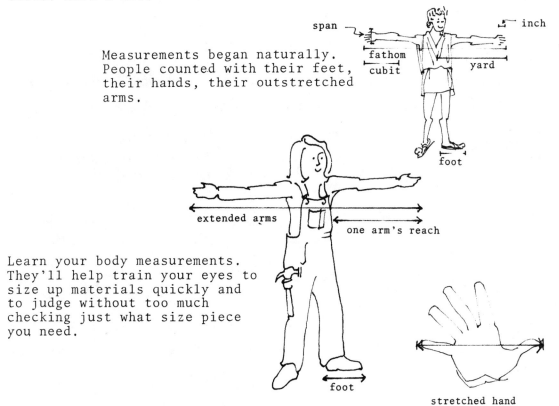

Measurements began naturally. People counted with their feet, their hands, their outstretched arms.

span

fathom

cubit

inch

yard

foot

extended arms

one arm's reach

Learn your body measurements. They'll help train your eyes to size up materials quickly and to judge without too much checking just what size piece you need.

foot

stretched hand

Keep Measurements Simple

Before 1850, few carpenters bothered to have their rulers marked with sixteenths.

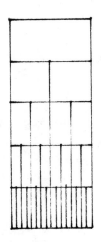

Today, fine carpenters still use round numbers, if possible.

Divide 1 inch in **2** and that's 2 $\frac{1}{2}$'s.

Divide 1 inch in **4** and that's 4 $\frac{1}{4}$'s.

Divide 1 inch in **8** and that's 8 $\frac{1}{8}$'s.

Divide 1 inch in **16** and that's 16 $\frac{1}{16}$'s.

Let Materials Guide You

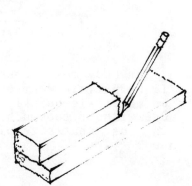

❖ Each board has three measurements--
a thickness, a width, and a length.
The thickness and width of boards
are about the same everywhere and
they have guided the planning in
this book.

❖ Planning is easier than sawing.

❖ Learn the standard sizes of boards--and how they fit together.
Think of them as building blocks. Avoid rip-cutting (cutting
to change thickness or width).

❖ Adjust projects to materials you have.

Let Projects Guide You

❖ Study the project you're beginning.
Ask yourself which dimensions matter,
which don't.

❖ Once you've begun, you can often
use the project itself to measure
other boards.

Learn Shortcuts

Try two methods for finding the point at the middle of this board.

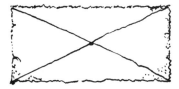

1. Measure its width, divide
   by two and mark that point.
   Then measure its length,
   divide by two and mark that
   point. Repeat the measurements if the points aren't
   close. This is the long way.

2. With your ruler, draw lines
   from the opposite corners.
   The 'x' crosses at the middle.
   This is the short way.

The instructions in the projects will teach you other shortcuts.

Common Sense

You need the measuring you learn in school. Learn to find those
eighths and sixteenths. But, for building, add to your ruler your
own built-in measurer--your common sense.

Metric Measurements... and why they're not in this book.

In school you've learned that metric measurements are important.
Many industries already use metric dimensions: the lumber
industry does not. Consider the problem:

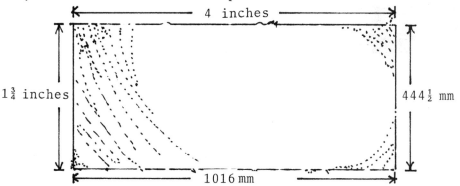

This is the end of a common board used everywhere in America.
Measure it both ways. The inch measurements will be clear....
But what about the millimeter measurement?

Can the lumber industry say, 'Use the same board, just use
these awkward measurements.' Or will the industry change the
sizes (and all its machines!) to produce even metric dimensions?
The choice is so difficult that it will not be made soon.

└SQUARE

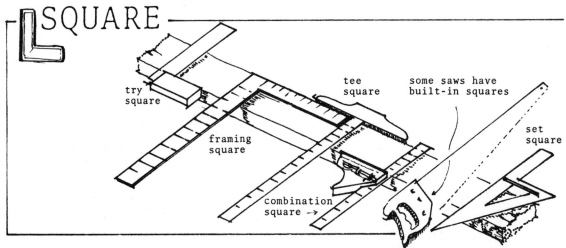

try square

framing square

tee square

some saws have built-in squares

combination square →

set square

The square is a tool so simple you might not notice its importance. But the Ancients who discovered it thought it was wonderful and even magical: it is a simple pattern that explains how to fit things together.

An Egyptian may have noticed it 4000 years ago while fishing in the Nile.

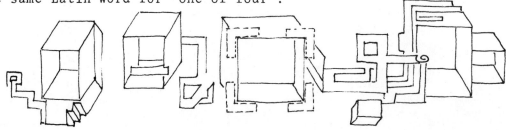

Or an ancient Greek may have found it by dividing a circle into four parts. The Greeks were especially curious about patterns that might explain how the world fitted together.

Today squares come in many styles: all squares allow you to draw the angle, the corner, that can be repeated four times to give you a perfect box. The words 'square' and 'quarter' come from the same Latin word for 'one of four'.

Squares today may be marked for measuring.

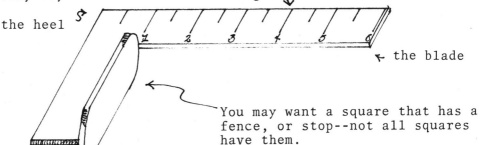

the heel

the blade

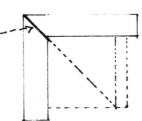

You may want a square that has a
fence, or stop—not all squares
have them.

Some squares have an extra angle,
which is the pattern for exactly
half a corner.

TO USE A SQUARE:
Marking:

Hold the stop against the edge of a board. Slide the square to
the point where you want to draw. Draw along the blade.

The square's pattern is called a 'right' angle. The word 'right'
here means 'straight and true.'

Testing or Trying:

Fit the square
next to pieces
you're putting
together to
check their
straightness.

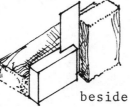

beside

outside

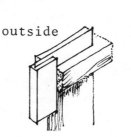

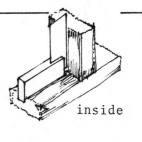

inside

If it's dropped, stepped on,
bent or knicked, its magic
may be lost. . . . .

Treat your square kindly.

OTHER TOOLS

Tools you'll need and probably already have. . .

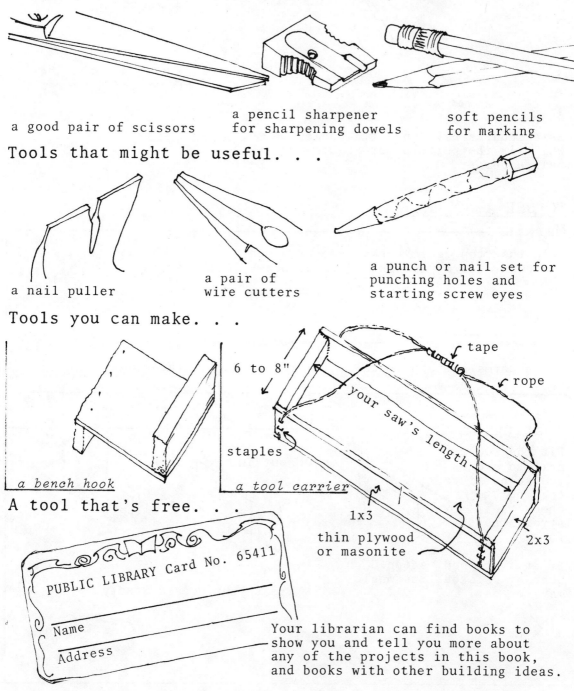

a good pair of scissors

a pencil sharpener
for sharpening dowels

soft pencils
for marking

Tools that might be useful. . .

a nail puller

a pair of
wire cutters

a punch or nail set for
punching holes and
starting screw eyes

Tools you can make. . .

a bench hook

6 to 8"

staples

a tool carrier

tape

rope

your saw's length

1x3

thin plywood
or masonite

2x3

A tool that's free. . .

PUBLIC LIBRARY Card No. 65411

Name

Address

Your librarian can find books to
show you and tell you more about
any of the projects in this book,
and books with other building ideas.

WOOD

Look around the room you're in. You can probably count a half dozen shapes, sizes and colors of wood. In the forest of wood products around you, you'll find it difficult at first to recognize the boards you need and can use to build with.

The projects in this book will start you off with simple lumber, a few boards that you will get to know well. You'll get to know some of these things:

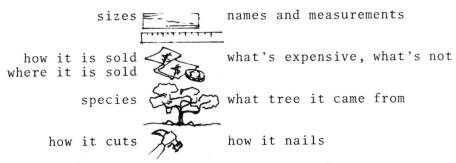

sizes	names and measurements
how it is sold where it is sold	what's expensive, what's not
species	what tree it came from
how it cuts	how it nails

What you learn about these few boards will teach you about other woods when you're ready.

Wood is the best teacher about wood.
Pick up a board, any scrap you can find.
That scrap has come a long way from its tree.
Still, each board remembers its tree.

Look at your board. The lines are its *grain*.
They're growth lines. The tree added a ring
each year it grew. Fat rings were good
growing years.

Notice how the grain looks different on the
edges, the faces, and the ends. The curved
grain on the end will help you picture the
section of tree the board was cut from.

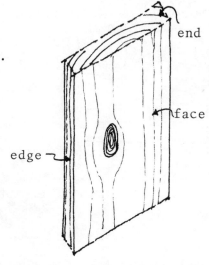

curved grain

rings

You may see darker wood from the inner part
of the tree, its *heartwood*, which died and
took on deeper color and strength as the
tree grew.

A missing edge may show you the round shape
of the tree.

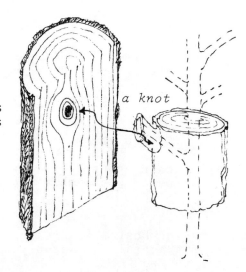

a knot

Dark circles, plugs or *knots*
show you where the young tree's
branches were grown over. Knots
may ooze a sticky goo called
pitch. Knots are hard. They'll
wiggle out sometimes. Look
closely. They have their own
grain, an end grain.

The living tree was full of moisture. Lumbermen remove most of it
by *air drying green, fresh-cut* boards in sheds for a long time or
by warming them in large ovens called *kilns*.

There are still traces of the tree's moisture. You can feel it in
boards fresh from the mill. You can smell it in some boards.

Drying shrinks wood.
Boards are named by their end measurements
when they're cut.

green size

actual size

Measure your board.
It will be smaller
than its name. Drying and *dressing* (smoothing)
took away the difference.

Your board will continue to dry.
It may bend up like a wet school
book drying out. Light growth rings shrink
more than dark ones, pulling at the edges.

Ends of boards dry fast and break, *shake* or *check*.

check

shake

You'll find ends painted to slow down this quick drying.

Your board is no longer alive, but it's still
changing: it has its own habits, its own
personality.

Learn to work *with* wood.
Learn what it likes to do,
what it doesn't like to do.
Let the wood teach you.

With a piece of fine sand paper,
polish a small spot on your board. Rub
hard. As you rub, the pattern of the grain,
its *figure*, will show clearer. Some boards
are prized for their bold colors or delicate
grains. But every board is special. Each board
lives in a tree unlike any other tree. Each
board reveals a little bit of nature's beauty.

LUMBER (how wood is sold)

Each board has a long official name: and a nickname:

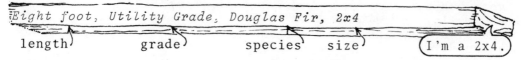

Eight foot, Utility Grade, Douglas Fir, 2x4

  length)   grade)   species size)   (I'm a 2x4.)

Lengths are simple. 8 feet is a standard length. You can buy longer (10 feet, 12 feet, 14 feet), and sometimes shorter (4 feet, 6 feet, 7 feet) lengths.

Species: Lumber yards often stock just one species at a time. You won't have to make a choice.

Grade: Take the 'lowest,' (least expensive) grade you can find.

Sizes: Learn these names, (1x3), and lumber sellers will know just what you're asking for. Learn these sizes. Drying and smoothing make actual sizes smaller than their names. Train your eye to recognize them. They'll guide every project you build.

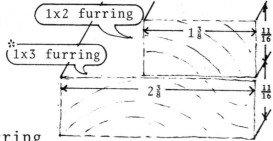

Furring

Sometimes called 'rough sawn,' it's often very rough. The least expensive wood, it may be sold in bundles of 10.

One Inch Stock

Smooth and straight stock. Expensive: three times as much as furring. Save it for special projects. Other widths: 8" 10" 12".

Molding solves problems: it covers corners, trims windows, holds carpet down and shelves up. Each type has a job for which it is cut out. You'll create new uses.

Named by their actual shapes,

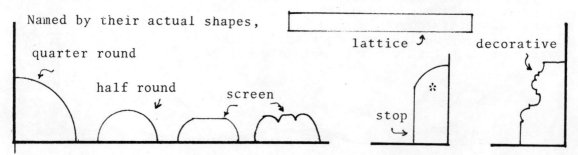

quarter round

half round

screen

lattice ↵

stop

decorative

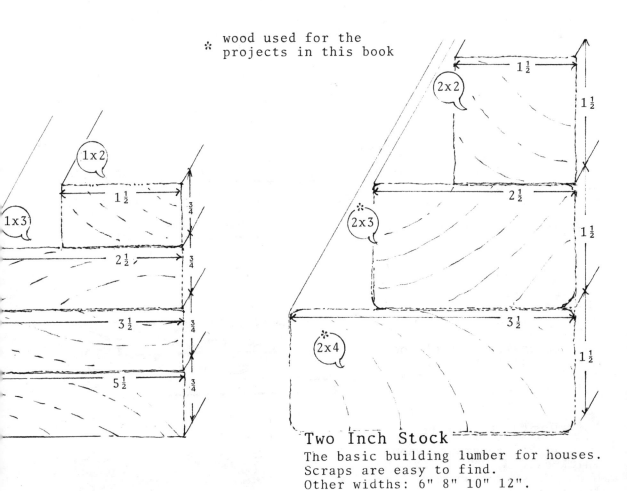

✻ wood used for the projects in this book

1x2 1½ ¾

1x3 2½ ¾

3½ ¾

5½ ¾

2x2 1½ 1½

✻ 2x3 2½ 1½

✻ 2x4 3½ 1½

Two Inch Stock
The basic building lumber for houses.
Scraps are easy to find.
Other widths: 6" 8" 10" 12".

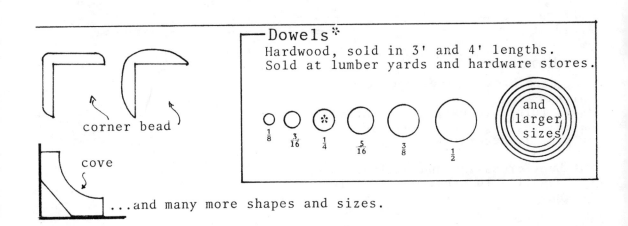

corner bead

cove

Dowels ✻
Hardwood, sold in 3' and 4' lengths.
Sold at lumber yards and hardware stores.

$\frac{1}{8}$ $\frac{3}{16}$ ✻ $\frac{1}{4}$ $\frac{5}{16}$ $\frac{3}{8}$ $\frac{1}{2}$ and larger sizes

...and many more shapes and sizes.

Sheet Lumber

Wood is sliced, or chipped, or chopped, or ground, then pressed and glued to make large sheets. The sheets are usually 4' by 8' when sold, a big size for you to handle. Look for scraps.

Plywood

. . . .a sliced wood sandwich
Thickness: $\frac{1}{4}$ $\frac{3}{8}$ $\frac{1}{2}$ $\frac{5}{8}$ $\frac{3}{4}$
Uses: construction, furniture, general building. Sold in many grades and styles, soft wood and hard wood. Usually named by its faces which may be smooth or rough. Collect all the plywood scraps you find.

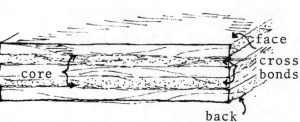

face
cross bonds
core
back

Waferboard

. . . .multi-colored wood chips
Thickness: $\frac{1}{4}$ $\frac{1}{2}$
Uses: Construction

Less expensive than plywood, it may be substituted for it when appearance isn't important. Cuts and nails well.

Particle Board

. . . .light tan ground wood
Thickness: $\frac{3}{8}$ $\frac{1}{2}$ $\frac{3}{4}$
Uses: Construction, countertops furniture.

Difficult to work with
Avoid it.

Hardboard

. . . .dark brown pulverized wood
Thickness: $\frac{1}{8}$ $\frac{1}{4}$
Uses: Furniture parts, decorative panelling, peg board. May have wood or plastic decorative face.

Not bad for sawing and nailing. Needs to be nailed to other wood to give it strength.

FINDING WOOD

. . .recycled wood saves for everyone.

Every neighborhood is different. Nobody's looks just like this. But
people in any neighborhood use wood and work with wood. Follow
these rules and you'll find your own special sources of the wood
scraps you need.

Neighborhood Store:
Some fruit or vegetable
boxes are part wood.

Neighbor who is
remodelling.

Neighbor who does building
or woodworking.

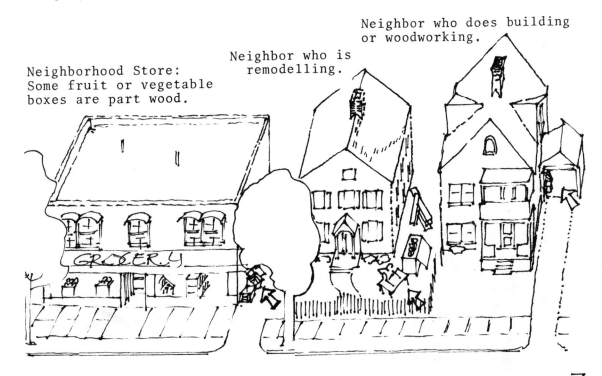

Rule 1: Don't be shy. Ask everyone. Everyone wants to build.
Everyone wants scraps sometimes. Everyone enjoys a polite request.

Rule 2: Be specific. Show people this list.
1. Any soft wood, any length: 1x3, 1x4, 2x3, 2x4
2. Plywood or hardboard, any thick-
   ness or shape.
3. Broomstocks, dowels, molding, any wheels.

Rule 3: Think of people who might bring wood when they visit:
your grandparents, cousins, etc.
Ask your parents which of their friends do woodworking.

Rule 4: Get help. Not many places will let you look for wood
without a grownup. They really are afraid you might get hurt.
Ask someone who likes to collect interesting things. Not everybody does.

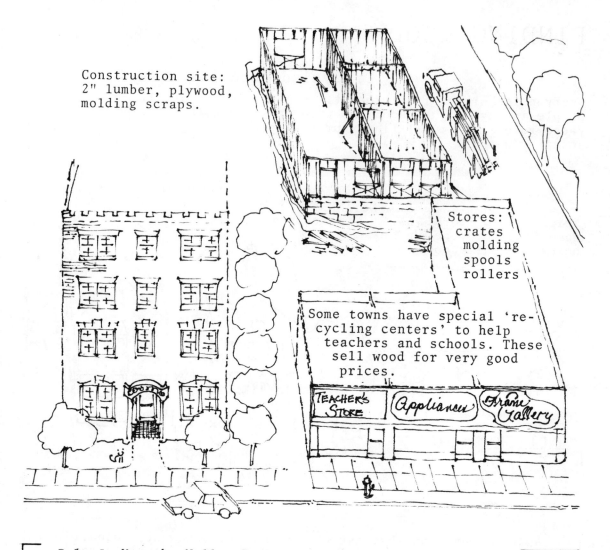

Construction site:
2" lumber, plywood,
molding scraps.

Stores:
crates
molding
spools
rollers

Some towns have special 'recycling centers' to help teachers and schools. These sell wood for very good prices.

TEACHER'S STORE

Appliance

Frame Gallery

Rule 5: Use the Yellow Pages: Look under these headings:
          Boxes-wooden
          Cabinet Makers
          Furniture: manufacturing
          Millwork
          Pallets and Skids
          Wood Turners
          Wood Workers

Rule 6: Never climb on a dumpster. Many have broken glass or metal. Some tip or close. Ask store owners or workers to put scraps aside for you.

Rule 7: Be patient. Be polite. People will remember you when you come back for more.

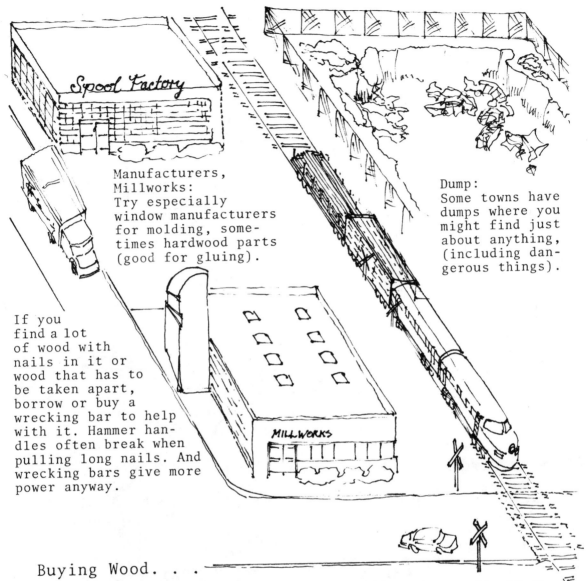

Manufacturers,
Millworks:
Try especially
window manufacturers
for molding, some-
times hardwood parts
(good for gluing).

Dump:
Some towns have
dumps where you
might find just
about anything,
(including dan-
gerous things).

If you
find a lot
of wood with
nails in it or
wood that has to
be taken apart,
borrow or buy a
wrecking bar to help
with it. Hammer han-
dles often break when
pulling long nails. And
wrecking bars give more
power anyway.

Buying Wood. . .

The wood business is changing. Lumber yards used to sell all the
wood in your town. Now, Building Supply Stores and even Department Stores sell wood. Find a place where sales people will be
helpful to a small customer like you. Ask people in your neighborhood where they buy wood and why.

You'll get the best service if you pick a time to go to the yard
or store when it's not busy. Avoid weekends and closing time.

If you're uncertain, take this book along and show the sales
person the project you want to build. Good sales people can be
helpful teachers.

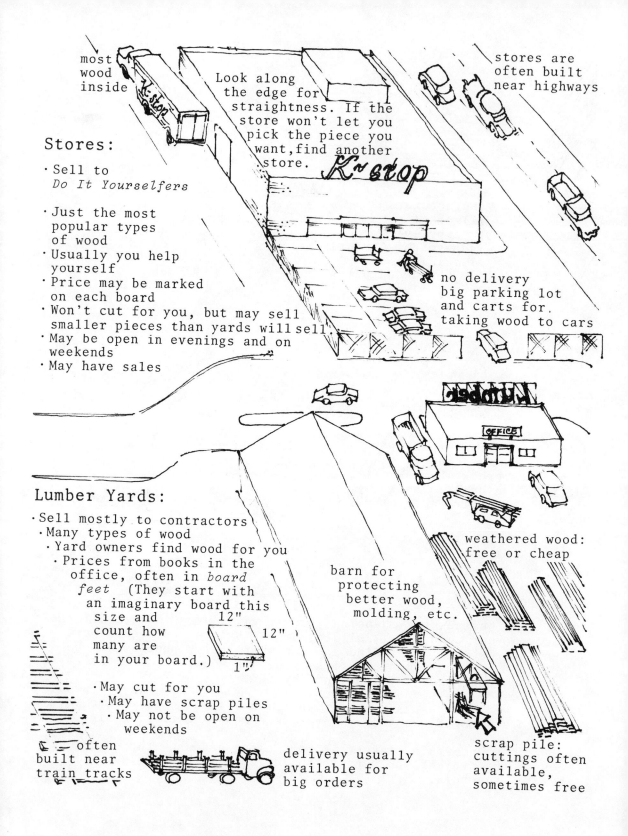

most wood inside

Look along the edge for straightness. If the store won't let you pick the piece you want, find another store.

K-stop

stores are often built near highways

Stores:

- Sell to *Do It Yourselfers*

- Just the most popular types of wood
- Usually you help yourself
- Price may be marked on each board
- Won't cut for you, but may sell smaller pieces than yards will sell
- May be open in evenings and on weekends
- May have sales

no delivery big parking lot and carts for taking wood to cars

Lumber Yards:

- Sell mostly to contractors
- Many types of wood
  - Yard owners find wood for you
  - Prices from books in the office, often in *board feet* (They start with an imaginary board this size and count how many are in your board.)

12" 12" 1"

- May cut for you
- May have scrap piles
- May not be open on weekends

often built near train tracks

delivery usually available for big orders

barn for protecting better wood, molding, etc.

weathered wood: free or cheap

scrap pile: cuttings often available, sometimes free

NAILS

Nails can be confusing: there are many types, many sizes and peculiar measurements. Most projects in this book use all-purpose nails, called Common Nails, because that's what they are...common and ordinary.

You will see many less-common nails. Remember that there is a hammer for every trade? Well, there are nails for every job too. You can learn about nails by looking at the jobs they do.

A RINGED FLOORING NAIL is used because it *won't* pull out.

A STAGING NAIL has a second head so that it *will* pull out.

An UPHOLSTERY NAIL is decorated to show off on finished work.

A BRAD has a small head that won't be seen on finished work.

STAPLES pinch screen or cloth tight.

INSULATED STAPLES won't crush electrical wires.

Look around your house. Can you find other nails that do special jobs? (Remember that the specialty of many nails is to be not seen.)

CHOICES

Long ago in England, nails were counted and sold.
Small nails were 100 for two English pennies, written 2d.
Large nails were 100 for ten English pennies, written 10d.

Sold by weight: scooped from bins

or in 1 pound or 5 pound boxes.

d for *danarius*, an ancient Roman coin

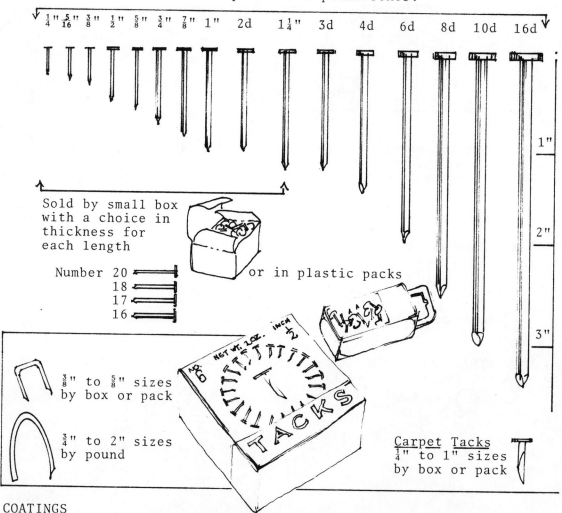

Sold by small box with a choice in thickness for each length

Number 20
18
17
16

or in plastic packs

$\frac{3}{8}$" to $\frac{5}{8}$" sizes by box or pack

$\frac{3}{4}$" to 2" sizes by pound

Carpet Tacks
$\frac{1}{4}$" to 1" sizes by box or pack

1"

2"

3"

COATINGS
Nails come with different coatings, *bright or hot-dipped, galvanized or blued,* for special purposes that won't make a difference to you. Ask for the least expensive.

CHOOSING A NAIL

To choose a nail, ask yourself: will it do the job?
Will it hold the boards without splitting them?

You won't always have the perfect size nail:
sometimes you can make almost-right nails work.

Short

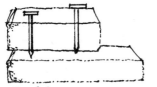      

Problem:
    boards come apart

More short nails
will not help. They
may split the wood
and make it weaker.

But gluing before
nailing may help.

Just Right

The general rules:

    for boards the same size,   for nailing small boards
                              to bigger boards,
                                go one to two thicknesses of the
                                thin board into the thick board.

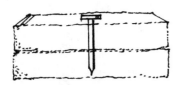   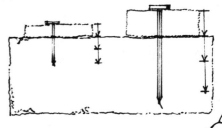

go almost all the way through.

Long

Problem:
    nails poke through...and big nails may split wood.

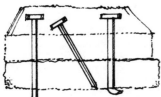   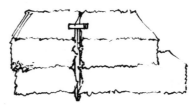

Drive the nail on an angle,
or turn the board over and
clinch the nail.

Flattening the point
may reduce splitting.

39

HOOKS AND EYES

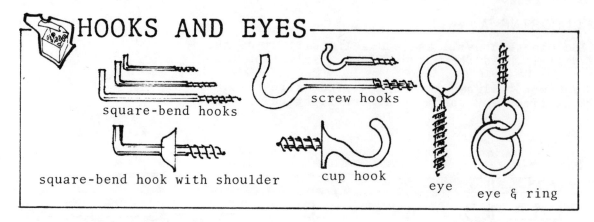

square-bend hooks

screw hooks

square-bend hook with shoulder

cup hook

eye

eye & ring

Hooks and eyes are members of the wood screw family. They're easy to use and solve problems that nails can't. They may be made of brass—the color of a penny, or of steel with a chrome finish —the color of a nickel.

Hardware stores sell eyes just large enough to push a string through or large enough to tie a ship to.

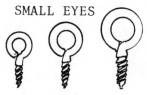

SMALL EYES

W216½ W214½ W212½

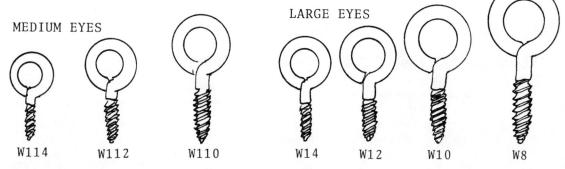

MEDIUM EYES

W114   W112   W110

LARGE EYES

W14   W12   W10   W8

These are the official names of some common screw eye sizes. It's not necessary to learn the numbers. Tell the person at the hardware store what you're trying to do and find an eye that looks right.

I want a screw eye this big that this dowel will fit through.

USING HOOKS AND EYES

Hammering crushes a screw eye.

A screw eye wants to be twisted.
Follow these steps and the eye's threads ——
will work for you not against you.

A. Make a pilot hole: start a nail, wiggle it loose. . .drive it
   in a little deeper, wiggle it out.

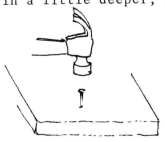 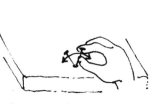 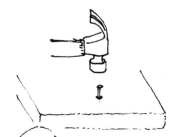

B. Rub soap on the threads for easier
   turning. Then start the hook or eye
   with your fingers. Turn it clockwise.
   Push in as you turn.

C. Use a lever to finish tightening it.

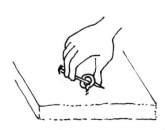  

   a nail   or the claw of your hammer

RECYCLE HOOKS AND EYES

Hooks and eyes twist out just as easily as they twist in. You
may find them on discarded wooden screens or old toys. Also re-
use them from projects you're finished with. A screw eye saved
is a screw eye you won't have to buy.

GLUE

The Ancient Egyptians used glue to hold up the decorations in their pyramids. Bee's wax, flour, tree pitches, egg white, fish, horns, and cheese have all been used in the search to make the perfect glue. Modern scientists have come very close with the glues you will use. These are based mostly on plastics, called polymers.

There are so many types of glue that you must teach yourself to read the labels and ask the questions that will tell you: will this glue do the job I want it to? Here's what you should find on the labels of the two glues you will use for the projects in this book.

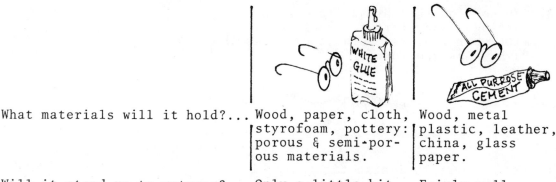

	WHITE GLUE	ALL PURPOSE CEMENT
What materials will it hold?...	Wood, paper, cloth, styrofoam, pottery: porous & semi-porous materials.	Wood, metal plastic, leather, china, glass paper.
Will it stand up to wetness?...	Only a little bit.	Fairly well.
How long can I keep it open?...	Ten minutes.	Not long: tube closes easily.
How long before it holds?......	30-45 minutes.	1-20 minutes.
How long before it's fully hard?.................	One day.	Two days.
How do I clean up any mess?....	Easily, with warm water and a rag.	Not easily. Get help. Use finger nail polish remover.
Is it dangerous?...............	No.	Yes. It burns, with nasty fumes. It marks some plastics.

42

TRICKS & TIPS

Experiment:

Using a glue will tell you even more than the label will. You'll develop a feel for just how strong it can be and how it holds best.

Glue is the most modern tool you'll use in this book. In the future, whole houses may be put together with it. Start studying it now.

Hold It:

The longer you can let the glue dry without the pieces moving, the better. Invent ways to hold pieces tight together.

weight   clamp   rubber bands   clothes pins   nail

A Thin Coat:

Instructions usually say 'Spread a thin layer.' This means that your pieces should fit so well that only a little glue is needed to fill the gap between them.

Everyone needs a fat layer sometimes. It's a little weak but it often works. Do clean up any dribbles with a rag before it dries.

The Stuffed Nozzle:

Even when you're neat and careful, glue containers get stuck up. Buy glue with simple spouts: its easier to clean.

use a nail or pin. . .   with plastic container, rap the nozzle with a hammer. . .

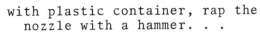

block of wood or bench edge

PAINT

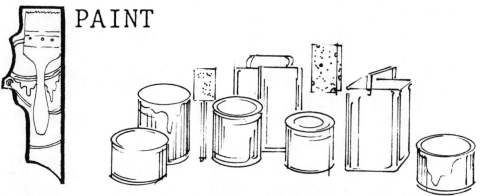

Shellac, laquer, wax, oil base paint, plastic base paint, stain, preservative: these are all *finishes*. They're used for

beauty

or protection

or both.

This is a book of hard *working* projects. They're not planned to be finished for beauty. That takes a lot of smoothing and sanding.

The projects that work in water could use a finish for protection.

Remember that all wood was once full of moisture? Unfinished boats and water wheels will soak moisture back up. Paint seals the water out.

GENERAL RULES:

1. Talk to your parents. *They'll have their own rules about painting. Remember, these paints won't wash out when they're dry.*

2. Work outside if possible. Less worry about mess. Fewer fumes.

3. Read instructions on cans.

4. Mix paint well...till you're bored.

5. Paint a thin coat. Wait an hour. Paint again. Dribbles and runs say you've tried to do too much in one coat.

Spray Paint:

*Buy for 'Quick Drying' paint.

*Your project must be completely dry.

*Keep the can upright as you work.

*Keep the can a foot away from your project.

cardboard box
for overspray

1 foot

newspaper

Clean Up:

*Turn the can upside down and spray four short blasts to clean nozzle.

*If you use paint thinner, ask a parent to help.

Latex Paint:

*Don't buy new paint. There are cans of latex paint with just a little left everywhere.

*Work should be almost dry.

*Dip the *tip*, not the whole brush.

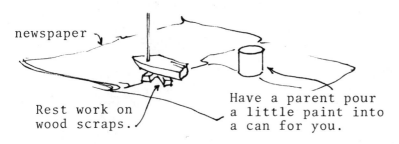

newspaper

Rest work on wood scraps.

Have a parent pour a little paint into a can for you.

PAINT BRUSH

Use an inexpensive 1½" wide plastic bristle brush.

Clean Up:

*Close paint tight.

*Wash up spills, brush, yourself with soap and warm water.

 # ODDS&ENDS

The projects in this
book need rubber bands,
bottlecaps, spools, and
spoons. Usually these
odds and ends are easy
to find at home, at a
neighbor's. Take note
of stuff that might
help you build or
invent as you clean
up your room or walk
home from school. You
might start a 'Savings
Place', a 'You Never
Know When You'll Need
One of These' place,
with boxes or cans to
organize the bits you
find.

You don't need
junk and you don't need
things you can get any
time, like hangers. You
do need a neat way of keeping
together the odds and ends that
are just waiting to solve a
problem in one of your
projects.

paper clips

washers

springs

bag ties

rubber bands,
pieces of elastic..

hobby sticks,
popsickle sticks,
tongue depressers,
swizzle sticks,
jack sticks..

canning
jar
lids

string, scraps,
thread, cord,
yarn..shoelaces,
fishing line..

spools, buttons,
tinkertoy parts..
wheels from broken
toys, lids, clothes
pins, marbles, washers..

nice cans or
plastic containers
are good for organizing.

PROJECTS

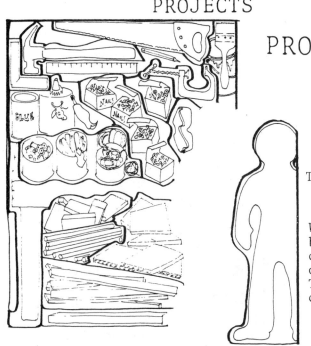

PROJECTS

PROJECTS

These projects are for *you*.

We've made them challenging
because we have a lot of
confidence in you. Your ways
of working are special.
Trust them and give them a
chance to work.

Give yourself chance*s*.

The first time through everything is awkward.
Try projects a second time.
You'll learn how much you've learned.

Find your own way. . .

We've offered *one* plan for putting each
project together.
We've asked: How can we keep sawing simple?
            Can we find easy positions for hammering?
            Can we leave room for adjustments?
Experiment: you may find better answers than we have.

Give yourself time.

Building takes time: more time than you guess it should.
You need time for mistakes, time for thinking.
Time for experimenting.
Every minute of it is *learning* time.

The Projects: Where Did They Come From. . .

This is a book about things that work. Children *everywhere* have *always* made things that work. When you make something work, you touch the experience of others who have made it work.

We chose projects
to put you in
touch with builders
of other lands:

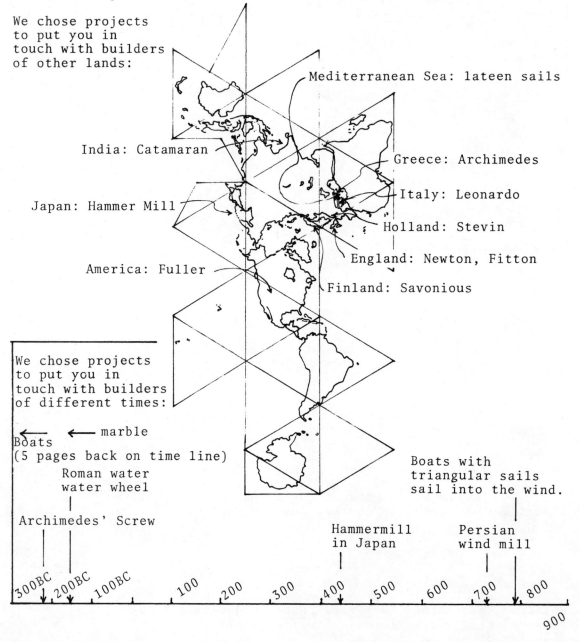

Mediterranean Sea: lateen sails

India: Catamaran

Greece: Archimedes

Italy: Leonardo

Japan: Hammer Mill

Holland: Stevin

England: Newton, Fitton

America: Fuller

Finland: Savonious

We chose projects
to put you in
touch with builders
of different times:

← marble
Boats
(5 pages back on time line)

Roman water
water wheel

Archimedes' Screw

Boats with
triangular sails
sail into the wind.

Hammermill
in Japan

Persian
wind mill

300BC   200BC   100BC   100   200   300   400   500   600   700   800

900

We chose projects to put you in touch with wind and water.

Wind and water are nature's teachers.
They have touched children everywhere, always.

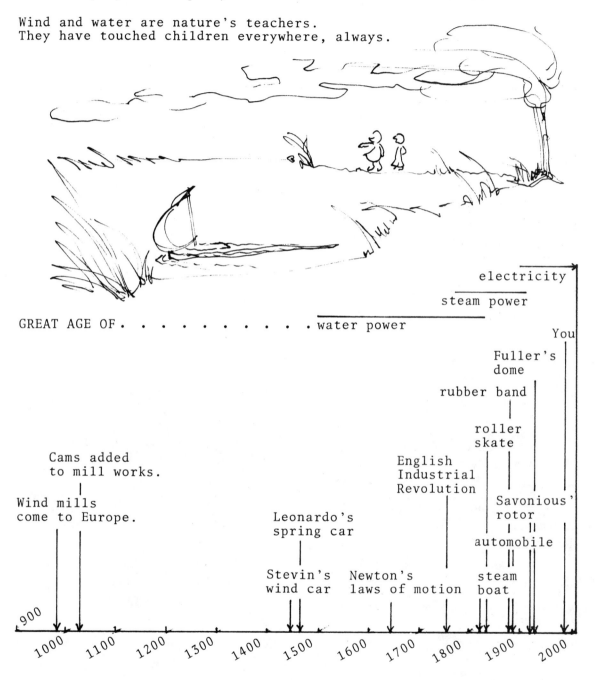

GREAT AGE OF . . . . water power

electricity

steam power

You

Fuller's dome

rubber band

roller skate

English Industrial Revolution

Savonious' rotor

automobile

Cams added to mill works.

Wind mills come to Europe.

Leonardo's spring car

Stevin's wind car

Newton's laws of motion

steam boat

900 1000 1100 1200 1300 1400 1500 1600 1700 1800 1900 2000

49

PROJECTS FOR PRACTICE

Give yourself a chance to practice hammering.
Practice can be imperfect: let nails bend, let boards split.
Relaxing makes learning easier.
Remembering that learning takes time makes it easier too.
Practice will build your muscles and co-ordination and, most
　　important, your confidence.

PURE PRACTICE

into the
end grain

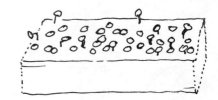

from a firewood pile
or a friendly tree surgeon

Start with a log or a block of soft wood. Make it steady.
Fill it with nails. Work until you can drive a 4d nail in
three or four strokes. That won't happen in one afternoon.
Come back to your practice block even after you've begun
other projects.

PRACTICE PROJECTS

make a spider

Spider Web:

4 pipe cleaners

Basket: make a border
of nails, weave string
or yarn around the nails.

nails and
rubber bands

plywood
scrap

round and round

Rattle: flatten bottle
caps on a block of wood. . .punch holes with
an 8d nail. . . . . . .attach with 4d
nails to a wood
scrap.

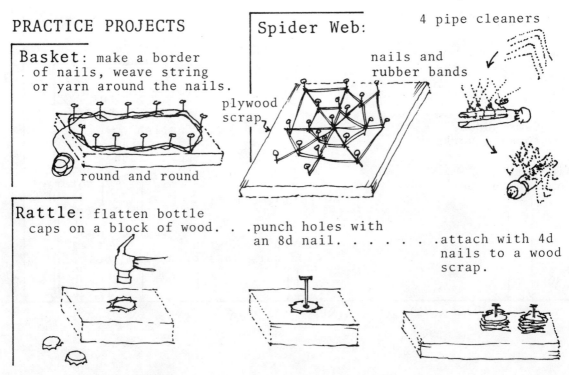

THE THAUMATROPE. . .quicker than the eye.

In 1826, Henry Fitton realized that the eye *held on* to pictures that moved quickly. He demonstrated this with the Thaumatrope, Greek words meaning *spinning wonder*. Fitton's little toy was the first in a chain of inventions that led to modern motion pictures.

Materials		
8" cardboard	1x3 2½"x2½"	or any scrap from the back of a tablet, for example
2	rubber bands	
2	8d nails	
	black magic marker	

A. Draw a bird on one side of your piece of cardboard. Draw a cage on the other side. Use heavy dark lines.

B. Punch holes with an 8d nail.

C. Attach rubber bands to the cardboard with lark's head knots (see Appendix I).

D. Start 8d nails in a scrap of 1x3.

E. Drop lark's heads over the nails.

Rubber bands should be stretched.

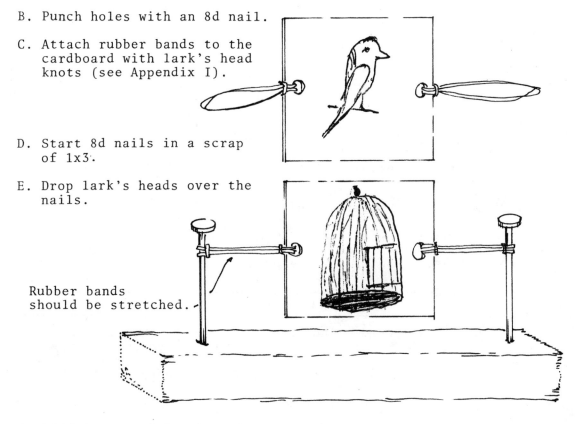

F. Wind it up and let it spin.
Can you think of other combinations of pictures?

PINBALL MACHINE

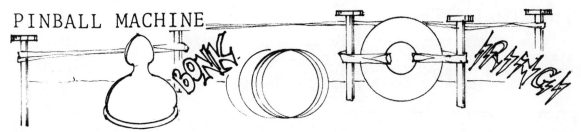

What is a machine? You know. But it's hard to put into words.
In dictionary words:

> machine, noun (from Latin: machina: device). Parts com-
>   bined to change or apply power or motion to do
>   some desired work.

Think about a pinball machine. the 'pin,' (a plastic spoon in
this design) is the striker. It applies the power and starts the
work. The bumpers and traps you set will change the motion of the
marble at work. Your design will shape the desired work.

Design your machine in two steps.

First set up your striker and the border around the board. Rest it
on a foot (a small board) but don't attach it. Test this with a
marble. Can you send the marble in
the direction you choose? How will
changing the board's tilt change
the motion?

higher lower

Then create problems for the marble to solve.
At each step, picture in your mind how the
marble will react. Then build your idea on
your board and test your guess. Make adjustments, then add another problem. Again:
imagine, build, test...imagine, build, test.

Some fourth graders have shared their machines to help to get
started. Try one of their ideas; then create designs of your own
completely different. Build a whole arcade.

Materials		. . .any size will do
any size	plywood or board	$\frac{3}{8}$ to $\frac{3}{4}$ inch thick: thick enough for your nails to stand strong without poking through
assorted	rubber bands plastic spoons marbles wood scrap odds & ends	choose to fit your design

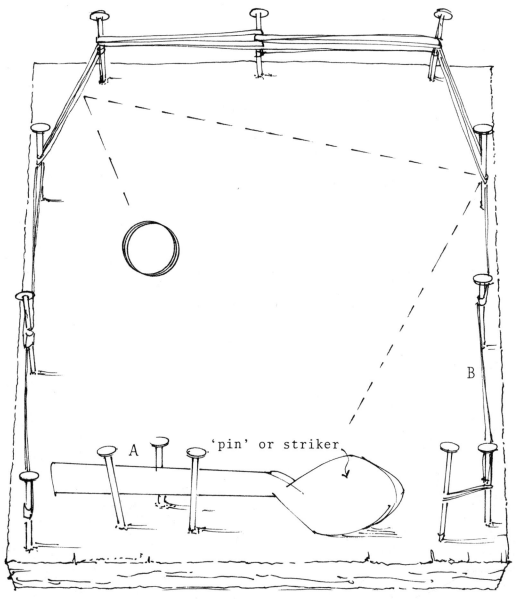

'pin' or striker

A

B

A. Get a rough idea in your head for your design. Place the spoon. Then pin it in place with 3 nails. Experiment until it flips freely.

B. Make your boundaries with nails and rubber bands. As you work, some of your first nails will fall out. Vibration causes this. Keep your board flat on the bench to prevent this.

C. Rest your board on a 'foot.' Test this work before you go on. Make adjustments. (Don't attach the foot 'til you're all through.)

DESIGNS

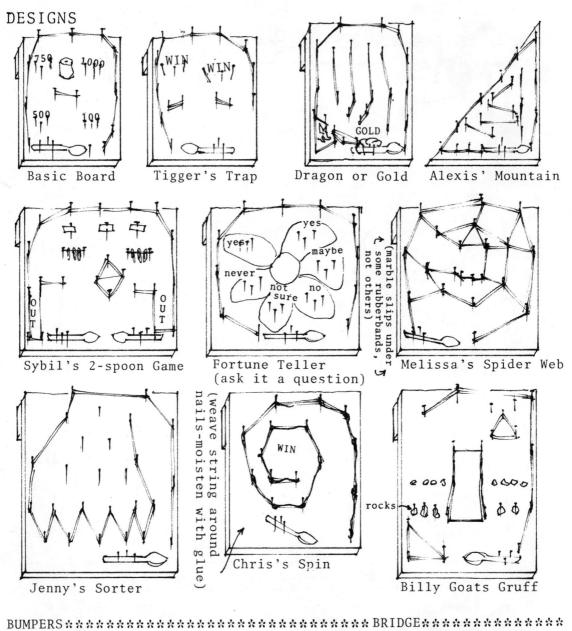

Basic Board

Tigger's Trap

Dragon or Gold

Alexis' Mountain

Sybil's 2-spoon Game

Fortune Teller
(ask it a question)

Melissa's Spider Web

(marble slips under
some rubberbands,
not others)

Jenny's Sorter

(weave string around
nails-moisten with glue)

Chris's Spin

Billy Goats Gruff

rocks

BUMPERS✵✵✵✵✵✵✵✵✵✵✵✵✵✵✵✵✵✵✵✵✵✵✵✵✵✵✵✵✵✵✵ BRIDGE✵✵✵✵✵✵✵✵✵✵✵✵✵✵✵

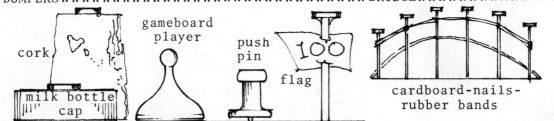

cork

milk bottle
cap

gameboard
player

push
pin

flag

cardboard-nails-
rubber bands

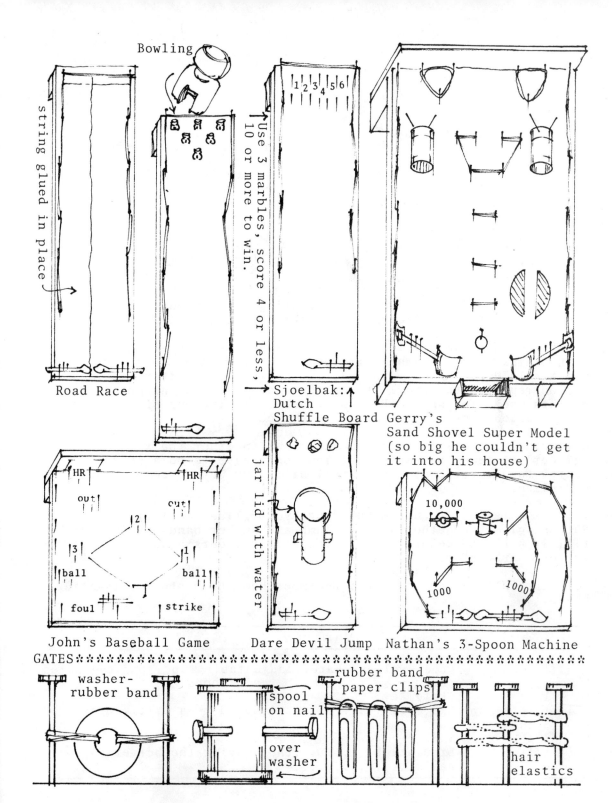

Bowling

string glued in place →

Road Race

Use 3 marbles, score 4 or less, 10 or more to win.

1 2 3 4 5 6

Sjoelbak: Dutch Shuffle Board

Gerry's Sand Shovel Super Model (so big he couldn't get it into his house)

HR   HR
out   out
3   2   1
ball   ball
foul   strike

John's Baseball Game

jar lid with water

Dare Devil Jump

10,000

1000   1000

Nathan's 3-Spoon Machine

GATES **

washer–rubber band

spool on nail

over washer

rubber band paper clips

hair elastics

55

EASY GLIDER

Joseph Marlin was the first inventor of the roller skate to make history. In 1760, he showed off his wooden skates on an English dance floor. Unfortunately, he couldn't turn. He crashed into a mirror.

J. L. Plimpton invented the modern roller skate in 1863. He added the center axle that allows skates to tilt and skaters to turn.

Plimpton's Axle

A. F. Smith of Chicago added ball bearings and speed. Skating became a craze for children and adults...more than 100 years ago.

After the building of smooth sidewalks--not as long ago as you might think--the next major improvement for roller skating came in the mid 1970's. Skates with plastic wheels and a better tilting action replaced the steel skates that your parents and grand-parents used. You should have no trouble finding one of those now unwanted steel skates for this project.

A young mechanic with an extra skate put together the first 'glider' at least 50 years ago. You don't have to be a good skater to use it. Coast down small hills. Or get up some speed and glide.

This is a lesson in custom building: your glider must fit you. Put the glider together with a clamp and rubber bands--adjust it till it's right--before you nail. Clever builders always find ways to test work before nailing.

Work carefully and be careful! Remember how the history of skating began.

Materials	
1	steel roller skate...adjustable type: try tag sales, bargain shops
1	skate key
4 ft. plus	2x3.................2x4 would be a little heavy
5 in.	2x3
3 ft.	1x3
1 ft.	broomstick.........the heavier the better
	nails..............4d

A. With a skate key, free the back half of a skate.

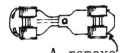

A remove

B. Attach that part of the skate to the 2x3
   (4d or 6d nails).

   Then hammer the heel of
   the skate to fit the 2x3.

start here→ B

←Put nails
in here too.

C. Cut: 2 pieces 1x3   10 in. long
         1 piece   2x3   5 in. long (or find a scrap)
         1 piece   broomstick   12 in. long

D. Start the seat. Nail (4d) the 1x3 pieces
   to both faces of the 2x3.

The Fitting ─────────────────

E. Attach the seat with your clamp.

F. Attach the broomstick with 2 or 3 rubber bands.

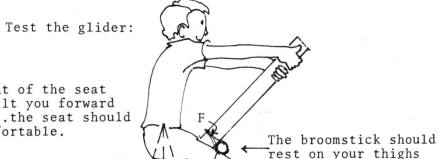

Test the glider:

The height of the seat
should tilt you forward
a little..the seat should
feel comfortable.

The center of your weight
should be a little ahead of
the skate wheel.

The broomstick should
rest on your thighs
without hurting.

Take your time. Try the seat and the support (broomstick) in two
or three positions.

The Assembly. . .when you're sure it feels ok.

E. Support the seat on the edge of your bench (with the clamp still in place). Fasten the seat with 3 nails (4d).

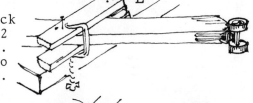

F. Test it again! Adjust the broomstick Now nail (6d) the broomstick with 2 nails. Broomstick can be stubborn. It may split a little. It may be so hard you'll need help with nailing.

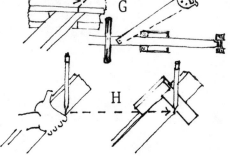

G. Trim off the front edges of the 1x3, cutting along the 2x3.

H. Now mark the point on the 2x3 that your hands hold when you test. Draw a cutting line with your square, and cut.

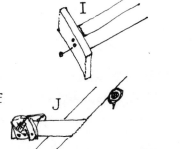

I. Nail a short piece of 1x3 (10 to 12 inches) across the end.

J. You may want to pad the seat and support. . wrap them with strips of old towel and tack it.

Get your skates. Find a safe, smooth place for the final test. And be careful.

On Your Own

Materials: a clip-on skate without teeth

In winter you could rebuild your easy glider for ice skating. Cut the end so the skate rests flat on the ice.

Adding a Sail

This is not for everybody. You need windy days...not every place
has them. And you need a large, paved playground, (not a parking
lot) so that you can follow winds wherever they blow.

The sail is a beach towel, or any piece of cloth large enough to
catch wind, but not too large to handle. The tacks will make very
small holes.

Materials		
	beach towel	30x60 is a common size; will not be cut
2 lengths of 5 ft.	1x3 or 2x3	length depends on towel size
1 length of 4 ft.	2x3	
	thumbtacks	or carpet tacks
	nails	4d

A. Cut 2 pieces of 1x3 the length of the towel.

B. Lay the towel out flat.
Lay the 1x3's along the edges.
Fold the towel around the 1x3.
Fasten with thumbtacks (every
8 inches or so).

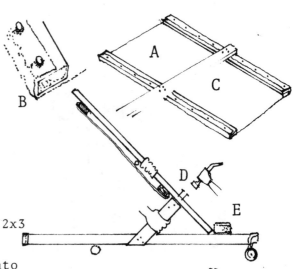

C. Nail (4d) the 1x3 next to the
top of the 2x3 mast first.

Stretch the towel as you nail
the bottom.

Now take the sail and glider
outside to nail together.

D. Lay the glider down. Nail the 2x3
mast to the back of the seat.

Have a friend hold the sail onto
the back of the seat.

E. Nail a block tight against the
mast's bottom. Can you see why
this is important?

F. Drive nails partway in, one at top of mast and one on
the base between the wheels. Stretch rope between them:
this is a 'stay' for support. Wait for the wind and be careful.

WOODEN RELATIVES

A scale is a measuring stick. A ruler is a one foot scale, for example.

There are other scales. A measuring stick that uses small measurements to stand for large measurements 'scales down.'

Most doll houses are built on a simple scale: 1 inch=1 foot.

In real life, most tables are 2½ feet tall.
A doll house table is 2½ inches tall.
When you build to scale, you make pieces to fit the new measuring stick you have chosen.

How tall are you?
How tall would you be in 1 inch scale?

			1x2
cork	clothespin	broomstick	steel wool hair
nails	draw-on faces	string hair	pipe cleaner arms
staple	string for hair	pipe cleaner arms	saw to make legs
string		cloth scrap skirt	thumbtack eyes
		tack eyes	staple nose

. . .at home

You may have a doll house, or you can make one out of boxes.
People, furniture, toys, decorations...all the things that
fill a house. Start with shapes that fit the scale, then trust
your imagination to fill in the details.

This is a good project for experimenting with all the uses of glue.

Materials		
assorted	broom sticks	
	wood scraps	1x2, 1x3, 2x3
	nails	4d, 8d
	tacks & staples	
	misc:	bottle caps, string, rubber bands, pipe cleaners, etc.
	glue	

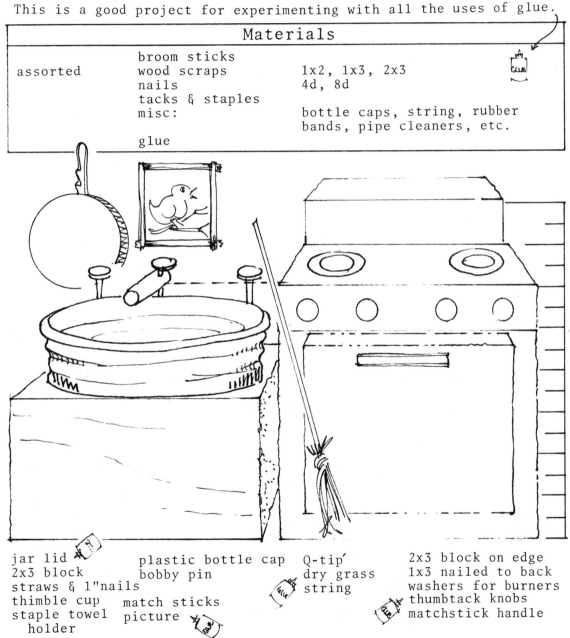

jar lid
2x3 block
straws & 1"nails
thimble cup
staple towel
  holder

plastic bottle cap
bobby pin

match sticks
picture

Q-tip
dry grass
string

2x3 block on edge
1x3 nailed to back
washers for burners
thumbtack knobs
matchstick handle

Another Scale

The waterwheel, hammer mill, mousetrap tractor, and some of the boats in this book are built on a 1" scale. You'll see this clothespin child at work on these projects.

These projects are <u>drawn</u> on a smaller than 1" scale. So the clothespin child will be drawn smaller than its normal size.

The clothespin is the key:
    picture it as a 4" clothespin—you'll see the size of the project you'll build;
    picture it as a 4' child—you'll know the size of a waterwheel or a hammer mill full size.

table	computer	chair		hammer:	nail
<u>table</u>	<u>computer</u>	<u>chair</u>		<u>hammer</u>:	nail
1x3 block	wood block	1x3			pencil eraser
8d nails	nails	4d nails		<u>saw</u>:	bobby pin
	string	rubber band		<u>goggles</u>:	paper clips bent
	matchbook	or string		<u>ruler</u>:	paper

BOATS

Water teaches. In the early Stone Age, a child climbed on a log floating in a river and discovered the first boat. When the log rolled, the child came up knowing the design needed work.

Seafarers have always been discoverers. They developed the arts of sailing and boat building faster than any of the land-based crafts. In the lessons of trial and error, the sea was quick to show their mistakes.

Buckminster Fuller, one of the great modern philosophers of invention, began his education watching ships and carving boats on an island off of Maine. He realized that all design should follow the principle of doing the most you can with the least amount of materials--wisdom of the shipbuilders.

Each boat you build will be an experiment. Water will be your classroom and teacher.

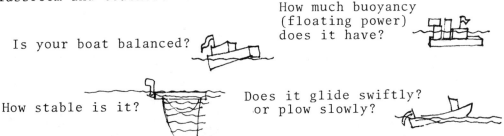

Is your boat balanced?

How much buoyancy (floating power) does it have?

How stable is it?

Does it glide swiftly? or plow slowly?

Start with simple designs. Build a fleet of boats. Test one against another. Don't expect to master boat building all at once. Remember: children have been working at it for 8000 years.

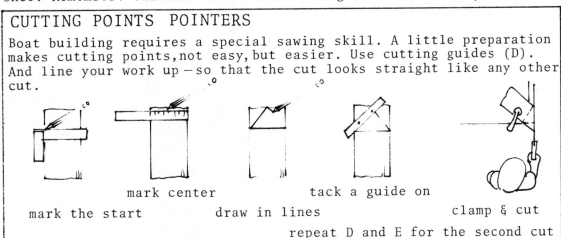

CUTTING POINTS POINTERS

Boat building requires a special sawing skill. A little preparation makes cutting points, not easy, but easier. Use cutting guides (D). And line your work up — so that the cut looks straight like any other cut.

mark the start

mark center

draw in lines

tack a guide on

clamp & cut

repeat D and E for the second cut

ON PAINT

You'll notice your boats getting heavier and heavier as you experiment with them. A coat of paint will seal water out. Let your boats dry for a day before you paint them.

BLOCK BOATS

This is the simplest and oldest
design for building boats..........
Study the board you choose to start with.
Float some scraps of 1x3, 1x4, 2x4, 2x6, any board you can find.
Poke at them. Which will be the least tippy? Which will glide easily?

Materials		
6-8"	1x4 or 2x4	work with scraps
8"	¾" stop molding or ¼" dowel	or other molding
odds & ends		for decoration
	paddle	
	nails	1" brads for molding or ½" staples for dowel
2 or 3	rubber bands	fat ones work best

the boat

A. Cut a point on your boat.

B. Attach molding or dowels to each side.

C. Work out your design. Add a wind screen cut from a clear plastic bottle, for example.

the paddle

D. Find a paddle...you may want to test more than one.

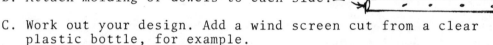

| wooden ice cream spoon | half a tongue depressor | 2 plastic spoons without handles glued together | other thin wood (from a fruit crate for example) |

E. Attach rubber bands to the paddle with lark's head around it.

or

assembly

Slip the paddle on the boat.
If it's loose, tighten it
with an extra turn
around the molding.

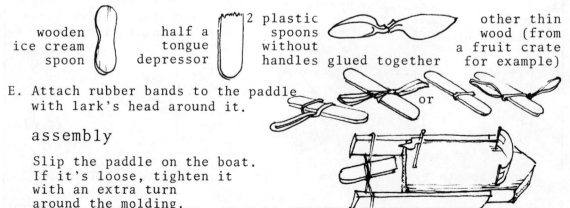

SAILS

Europe

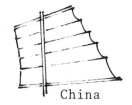
China

Vietnam

Hawaii

Sails evolved to suit the boats, winds, and materials of every part of the world. Sail makers have used leaves, animal skins, mats of reeds, linen, cotton, and synthetic fibers.

Cut your sails from plastic shopping bags. They meet the sail maker's tests: they're abundant, light, easy to work with, and a bonus- waterproof. Adapt this basic plan to create sails of any size and shape.

Materials . . .for a basic triangular sail
plastic shopping bag
string
plastic tape — electrician's tape, for example
¼" dowel — or plastic straw for booms of small sails
paper clip
toothpicks

A. Make pattern out of newspaper. This will save you time and trouble.

B. Lay the pattern on your plastic. Cut the sail 1" larger than the pattern, on edges to be folded.

C. Trim off corners for easier folding. Cut a couple slits in the curved edge.

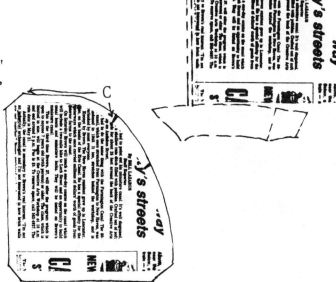

D. Attach a paper clip to the
   boom with tape.

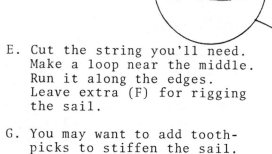

E. Cut the string you'll need.
   Make a loop near the middle.
   Run it along the edges.
   Leave extra (F) for rigging
   the sail.

G. You may want to add toothpicks to stiffen the sail.

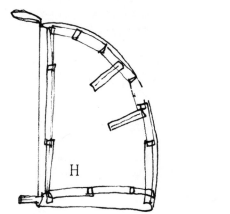

H. Fold over and tape each edge.
   Plastic is slippery. Find a
   helper to hold everything in
   place while you are working.

Simple Lug Sail

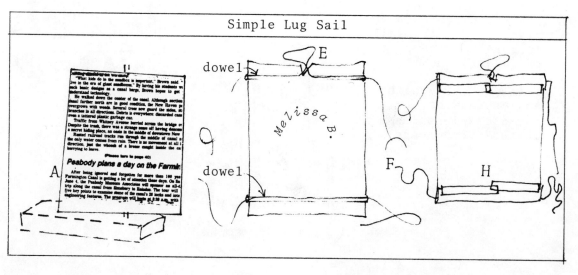

HULLS . .

Early in history, boat builders learned that
hollowed out logs made better boats than solid logs.
They began to build hulls. Think of the shape of a
walnut shell or hull.

Hulls require more work than solid block boats. But race a rubber
band hull against a rubber band block boat and discover the difference. The design below shows one combination of materials that
fit together. The combinations don't match perfectly, but they
will give you a good start at water-tight boats.

Materials		
approx. $3\frac{1}{2}$"x8"	$\frac{1}{8}$" or $\frac{1}{4}$" plywood	a good use for panelling scraps
16"	$\frac{3}{4}$" stop molding	
5"	1x3 furring	if you have full 1x3 stock, use it here
	waterproof glue	see GLUE
	nails	1" brads

A. Cut 2 pieces stop molding, 8" long.
   1 piece   1x3,   2" long.
   1 piece   1x3,   3" long.

B. Pinch the molding and the 1x3 pieces to
   make a pattern for the bottom. Draw around
   it. Cut this piece.

C. Put glue on all edges where wood will meet wood.

D. Clamp the pieces together with rubber bands.
   Put a weight on it so that all
   edges are pressed together.
   Let the glue dry — read the
   instructions on the tube. Be patient.

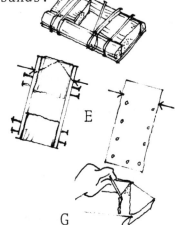

LATER

E. Mark a point on the longer end.
   Add nails to the edges and bottom.

   Don't put nails in the path your
   saw will cut when you cut the point.

F. Cut the point.

G. With a toothpick, seal the seams
   with extra glue.

Now that you've got the basics, some variations. . .

RUBBER BAND RACER

Build a hull with extra long side pieces. See steps under BLOCK BOAT for building and attaching a paddle.

SAILBOAT

A. Attach mast with 2 nails and string and a few drops of glue, or a spool glued to the bow.

B. Use a sail with plastic straw booms.

C. Cut a big rudder from a plastic lid. Attach to dowel with rubber band.

LEONARDO'S PADDLE BOAT

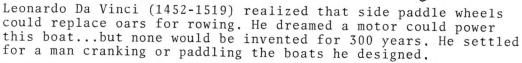

Leonardo Da Vinci (1452-1519) realized that side paddle wheels could replace oars for rowing. He dreamed a motor could power this boat...but none would be invented for 300 years. He settled for a man cranking or paddling the boats he designed.

Materials		
2	tongue depressors	from drug store, or
6"	¼" dowel	your doctor
2	screw eyes	
	small spool	
	cotton thread or light string	
3 or 4	rubber bands	

A. Mark point for screw eyes with your square. Put screw eyes in.

B. Put the dowel through the screw eyes. Lash the tongue depressors to both sides with thread. Then glue generously.

C. Nail the spool to the bow. It should turn.

D. Make a chain of 3 or 4 rubber bands. Attach one end to the dowel axle with a tight lark's head. Wrap the chain around the spool and hook the other end to a nail in the stern.

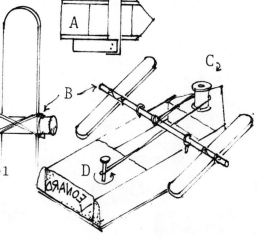

NEWTON'S STEAMBOAT

Isaac Newton (1642-1727) explored the mechanics of light, gravity and numbers. He didn't invent a steamboat. He did give to science the law of motion that this boat demonstrates:

"For every action, there is an equal and opposite reaction."

Materials		
	empty 4 oz. oil can	ask around your neighbor-hood--its a common size
4	short candle nails	6d

A. Make the hull with a 3" hold.

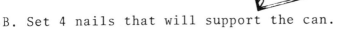

B. Set 4 nails that will support the can.

C. Wash the can with dishwashing soap and warm water. Squeeze any left over oil out.

D. Then squeeze the can, dunk the nozzle in water, and release.

squeeze   release

It will draw water in--only a tablespoon or 2 of water.

Lexie B.

E. Trim the candle so that the flame just touches the can. Test this boat on smooth water, with no winds to challenge its tiny power. Be patient...and be careful.

DESIGN & DECORATION

The plans in this section concentrate on making boats work. Don't limit your designs. Boats are built to do a job: to fish, to carry passengers, to carry cargo, to live on, to race. Look at boats (if you live near water) or find a book on boats. Build a fishing boat, an oil tanker, a tugboat, a houseboat. Discover why each boat takes its shape.

Seafarers decorate their boats just as you decorate your room. To make it unique and personal.

eyes to see danger

names of sea spirits or loved ones

sails to identify

CATAMARAN

The catamaran (Fr. Indian: *katta*=tie, *maran*=tree), belongs to the raft family. Its outriggers began as solid logs. Modern catamarans have light fiberglass hulls. Like their ancient ancestors, they're a simple, stable, easy to sail craft.

This Coffee Can Cat is easy to build. Rig it with a large sail, and it will glide with the slightest breeze. It's a stable boat in any water.

Materials		
4	1 pound coffee cans with plastic lids	If no one in your family drinks coffee, don't fret. There's one coffee drinker in every neighborhood.
10" approx.	1x3	
4"x10" approx.	$\frac{1}{4}$" or $\frac{3}{8}$"plywood	for the deck: if you have no scraps of plywood, use more 1x3
3'	$\frac{1}{4}$" or $\frac{3}{8}$"dowel string	
1 more	plastic lid molding scrap nails	$\frac{1}{2}$" tacks, 1" brads, $\frac{1}{2}$" staples

A. Cut the deck and the crossbeam (1x3) the same length. Nail the deck to the edge of the 1x3.

B. Attach the 4 lids with tacks, two to each side of the crossbeam.

C. Attach a 25-30" mast with staples.

D. Attach a large, smooth plastic lid (rudder) to a 9" dowel or molding scrap (tiller) with tacks.

E. Put 2 nails in the deck to hold the rudder. Double over a rubber band to hold it in place.

F. Add 'stays,' ropes that give extra support, to the mast.

G. Pop the coffee cans into their lids.

H. Rig it with a large sail.

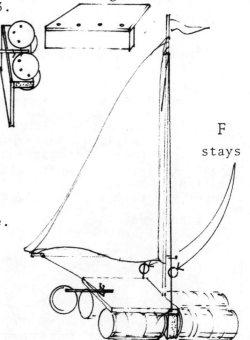

F
stays

TEST POND

A test pond will allow you to study and rework your boats, before you hike to a pond or stream. It's more economical than filling the bathtub every time you need a test. If you can borrow a wading pool, you can skip the following and go straight to sailing.

Find a level space, where winds blow, that you can reach with a garden hose. You will know if the space is level after you fill the pond. To save work, find out before. Borrow a level or make a leveling tool with a straight board and a small glass of water.

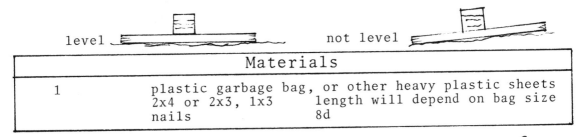

level   not level

Materials		
1	plastic garbage bag, or other heavy plastic sheets	
	2x4 or 2x3, 1x3	length will depend on bag size
	nails	8d

A. Cut 2 seams of the garbage bag to make a large sheet.

B. Make a frame 10 inches shorter than the sheet is wide, and 10 inches shorter than it is long.

The boards should rest on their edges.

C. Smooth the ground.
   Check for level.

D. Lay the plastic over the frame. The frame and the ground, not the plastic liner must carry the weight of the water. Fill in any low spaces with dirt.

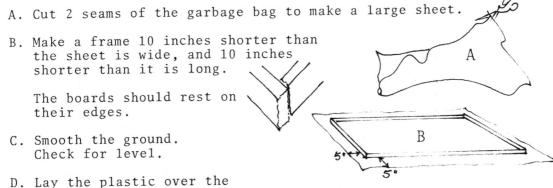

E. Fill your pond and begin your explorations.

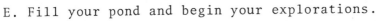

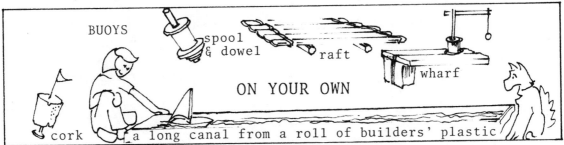

BUOYS

spool & dowel   raft

wharf

ON YOUR OWN

cork   a long canal from a roll of builders' plastic

WIND CAR

Inventors dreamed of creating a self-propelled vehicle for hundreds of years before the first gasoline powered car sputtered onto the road in 1885.

The early dreamers lacked a Prime Mover. People or animals are Prime Movers.

But both tire, and their appeal and power are limited.

Wind was the first big Prime Mover men had put to work. In the Middle Ages, improved sails had replaced oarsmen on ships and set off the Age of Discovery. It was natural that someone would try Wind as a Prime Mover for a land car.

Stevin's Wind Car

Marco Polo had seen sails on carts in China in 1295. Simon Stevin, (1548-1620), a mathematician, built a sailing car in Holland--the land of strong winds and expert sailors.

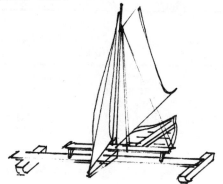

Stevin's car never caught on. The Dutch did develop a sister invention--the Ice Boat--which sped along their canals in winter. Ice boating is still a popular sport. The Wind Car might have been more practical if there had been roads as flat and smooth as canals. Wind cars were tried later, on special roads of rails, but those belonged to another Prime Mover, the first self-propelled vehicle: the Steam Engine.

Materials		
12"	1x3	or 1x2
1	roller skate	see Easy Glider
1-36"	$\frac{1}{4}$" dowel	
2-36"	$\frac{1}{8}$" dowel	or $\frac{1}{4}$"
1	garbage bag	medium size
	plastic tape	
4	rubber bands	
1	screw eye	
	glue	
	string	
	nails	8d
	$\frac{1}{2}$" staples	
	skate key	

THE WHEELS AND AXLES

A. Take the wheels off a skate. You'll need 2 skate keys. A wrench or a pair of pliers may be easier to find.

B. Most skate wheels will fit snugly on a $\frac{1}{4}$" dowel. Cut 18" of $\frac{1}{4}$" dowel for the rear axle. ($\frac{1}{2}$ of a 36" dowel--save the other half for the mast).

C. Start the wheels onto the axle. Tap gently to work them all the way onto the axle.

D. For the front axle, use the axle from the skate, or a 4" piece of dowel. Use one wheel.

THE HULL

E. Cut a piece of 1x3 or 1x2, 12" long.

F. Start 2 8d nails in the end of the 1x3, to support the front axle.

G. Start 2 8d nails in the middle of the hull, to support the mast.

H. Attach rear axle to the bottom of the hull, with 3 $\frac{1}{2}$" staples.

I. Attach the front axle to the nails with rubber bands lapped over and over.

J. Tie an 18" mast to the nails. Tie clove hitches the length of the nails. Add a few drops of glue.

THE SAIL

You'll need a big sail. This triangular *lateen* sail will run both with and across the wind.

K. Use 2 36" dowels to lay out the sail.

L. Attach small, strong rubber bands to the booms.

M. Put a stick through the rubber bands to hold the booms in place while you are working on the sail.

N. Finish, as in SAILS.

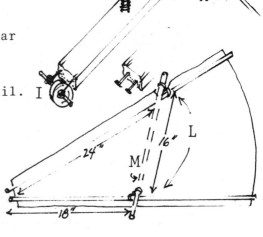

73

ASSEMBLY

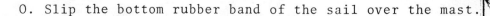

O. Slip the bottom rubber band of the sail over the mast.

P. Loop the top rubber band of the sail over and over the mast, until the sail holds tight.

Q. Punch a hole with a nail and tie a string round the boom (for controlling the sail).

R. Support the car on a block. Set a screw eye in the stern.
Tie the boom string to the screw eye.

S. Attach a stay (string) from the top of the mast to the screw eye.
LOOK FOR SMOOTH PAVEMENT AND LIVELY WINDS.

A SMALL LESSON ON A BIG DISCOVERY

The first sailors ran with the winds--simple enough if you can wait for the right wind.

With the lateen sail, sea farers could zig-zag into the winds. Sailors could travel in any direction they chose. World exploration began.

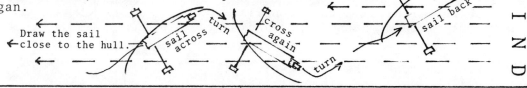

Draw the sail close to the hull.

sail across   turn   cross again   turn   sail back across

W I N D

ON YOUR OWN: AN ICE BOAT

Use metal lids from cans for runners. Design a hull that you can nail the lids to easily.

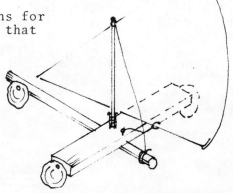

MOUSETRAP TRACTOR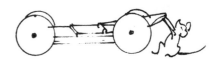

Leonardo Da Vinci designed history's first wind-up car in the
1490's. Clock makers had improved the art of making springs.
Leonardo put their springs on a cart.
He knew the limitations of wind-up
cars as well as you do: when the
spring unwinds, the car stops.
Leonardo put two springs on his
cart. While one spring moved
the cart, the driver cranked
up the other. With all this

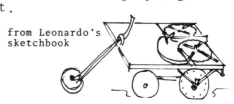

from Leonardo's
sketchbook

cranking, it's hard to say that Leonardo replaced man as the
Prime Mover.

Spring power was impractical. But in his studies, Leonardo drew
roller bearings, 3-speed gear transmissions and a differential
transmission--all necessary for the development of the modern
automobile, 400 years later.

Clockwork motors went into toys--for princes and princesses, at
least, in Leonardo's time. Inventions often appear first in toys.
They grow with the imaginations of the children they entertain.
The Chinese used gunpowder for firecrackers; the Greeks made pup-
pets dance by steam power. Toys teach.

The Mousetrap Tractor explores a problem that clock and automobile designers had to solve. The release of power must be
controlled. The wire added to the mouse trap and the large
wheels slow down the spring's release. A quick release would
spins the wheels in place.

Note the weight is important: a lighter car will move faster and
farther. Henry Ford knew this. But the American automobile industry he founded ignored this for many years. Today their designers are again building lightweight cars.

Materials		
1	mousetrap	
8"	1x3	or lighter wood if you can find it
4	plastic lids	from 1 lb. coffee cans
1	wire coat hanger	
2- 5"	$\frac{1}{4}$" dowels	
20"	string	
4	screw eyes	
	tape	
	glue	plastic cement
	nails	1"

THE CHASSIS

A. Cut a piece of 1x3, 8" long."

B. Mark lines $\frac{1}{2}$" from each end.

C. Set screw eyes, $\frac{1}{4}$" from each edge.

THE MOTOR

D. Cut 5" of the elbow of a wire hanger.

Clamp the hanger between a board and your bench--right on the lines you want to cut.

Now, grasp the rest of the hanger, and bend it up and down until the wire breaks...or borrow a wire cutter.

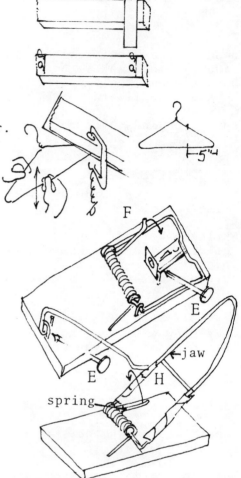

E. Study your mouse trap. Most look like this one.

All springs either push (like a ballpoint pen spring), or pull (like a screen door spring). Is this a pushing or pulling spring?

With a nail, pry the *trigger* pieces off.

F. Lift the end of the *spring* with the tip of a finger nail. This will make attaching the wire easier.

G. Now tape the hanger elbow to both sides of the jaw. Make a tight, neat job of this.

H. Finally, lift the spring back over the jaw with a nail.

THE WHEELS

Wheels are always hard to find. For this project, the coffee can lids are a good size and weight.

I. Most plastic lids have a mark from the machine that made them at their center--a sort of belly button. Rub the lid with a finger tip to find it. Punch a hole with a nail through that spot, on all four lids.

J. Cut 2 $\frac{1}{4}$" dowels, 5" long. Taper their ends slightly with a pencil sharpener.

K. Nail the trap to the chassis, $\frac{3}{4}$" from the end, with 2 1" nails.

L. Slip the axles through the screw eyes.

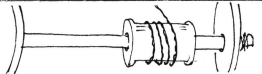

OPTIONAL: TWO-SPEED TRANSMISSION

A small spool on the power axle will allow your car to unwind at 2 speeds. Wrap tape on the axle so the spool will fit tight.

M. Cut 20" of string--that will give you plenty for knots and allow the car to coast after the spring is spent.

N. Attach one end to the wire, the other end to the power axle, with 4 clove hitches.

O. Work the wheels onto the axles carefully. If the wheels need extra support, wrap string around the axle and moisten with glue.

P. These wheels will always be 'delicate.' To wind: push the spring back and hold it with one hand, spin the axle to take up the string.

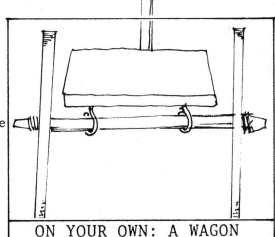

ON YOUR OWN: A WAGON

FLAG POLE (very tall)

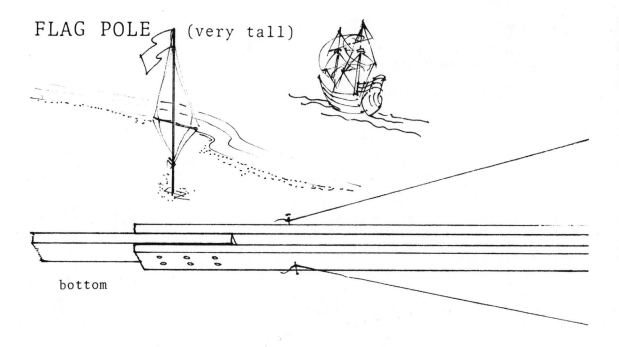

bottom

This flagpole stands tall without heavy, expensive materials. It's 'rigged' like a boat mast. The slender 1x3's are held straight by a crossbar and stays.

A small pulley would be fun, but an inexpensive screw eye works just as well.

An old pillowcase or sheet will make many flags. Those shown below are from the International Flag Code that ships use. Find more in an encyclopedia.

When you get tired of your flagpole, remember, the wood can be used again in many other projects.

Materials		
3	1x3's	(or 1x2's), 8 ft. long
3 ft.	1x3	(or 1x2)
4 ft.	2x4	(or 2x3)
40 ft.	heavy string	or light twine
2	spring clothes pins	
	old sheet or pillow case	
1	screweye	

A. Pick the straightest 1x3 for the top section. Sandwich about 15 inches of it between 15 inches of the other 2 1x3's. Use 6 nails for each side.

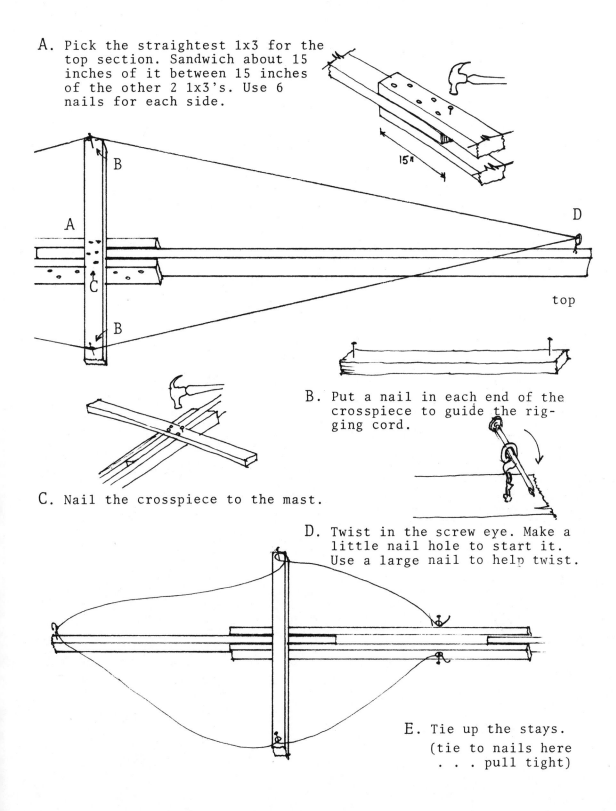

15"

B

A

D

C

B

top

B. Put a nail in each end of the crosspiece to guide the rigging cord.

C. Nail the crosspiece to the mast.

D. Twist in the screw eye. Make a little nail hole to start it. Use a large nail to help twist.

E. Tie up the stays.
(tie to nails here
. . . pull tight)

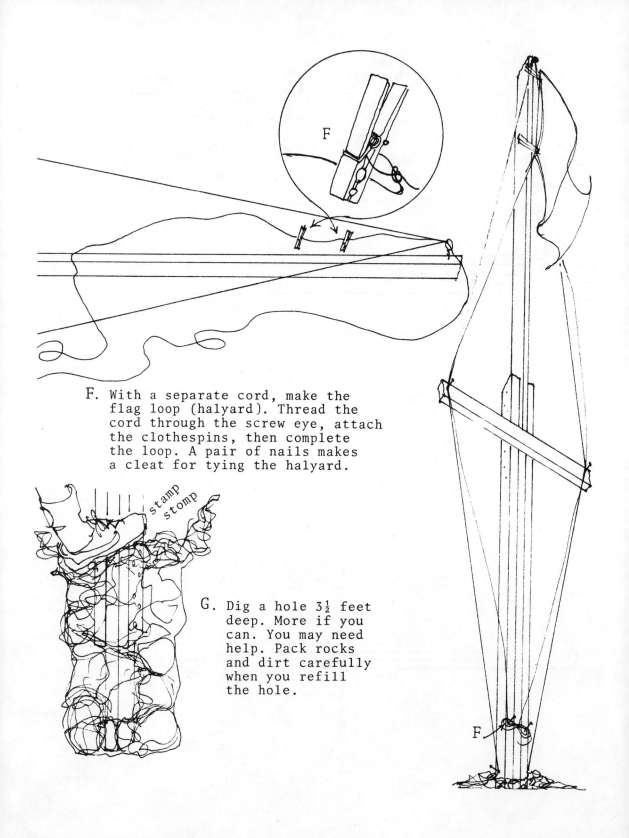

F. With a separate cord, make the
flag loop (halyard). Thread the
cord through the screw eye, attach
the clothespins, then complete
the loop. A pair of nails makes
a cleat for tying the halyard.

stamp
stomp

G. Dig a hole 3½ feet
deep. More if you
can. You may need
help. Pack rocks
and dirt carefully
when you refill
the hole.

DYMAXION TENT

In kindergarten, you built with blocks
shaped like these.

Your buildings probably looked like this. . .

In 1928, Buckminster Fuller began to experiment
with building blocks shaped like this.

For the past fifty years, he has built
buildings shaped like this. . .

He would want you to discover the difference between the two
types of building blocks.
Experiment. You'll need straws cut in half, and pipe cleaners.

Build a cube: and a tetrahedron:
 (12 straws)   (6 straws)

Give each a push. Which collapses? Which stands? Why? Can you
build a simpler stable building block than the tetrahedron?

Fuller has spent his life looking for designs in which the
least amount of materials do the most amount of work. His most
complex ideas begin with the simple tetrahedron.

Tents are *most for least* shelters. People who carry their houses
care about weight. You care about materials. This project's
tetrahedron-based frame makes a nice play space using only a
little wood.

Materials		
8-8' (60 feet altogether)	1x2's or 1x3's	You might use other wood, like tomato stakes.
9	4" plastic lids or 6" squares of carpet	cut from scraps
1 sheet	8' by 12', 6mm polyethelene film	builders' plastic
or 2	bed sheets	ready to be thrown out
1 box	⅝" carpet tacks	
1 pack	thumb tacks	
(You can use all this wood and plastic for other projects when you're tired of the tent.)		

Build a Model

Architects and engineers build scale models to study their designs. Use your straws and pipe cleaners to build a model of the tent. Follow the steps below that you will use to put together your tent.

On your model, can you fill in the tetrahedrons, four of them, that give the frame strength?

THE BONES

A. Cut 15 4' pieces of 1x2 (or 1x3).

B. Find 9 *hubs:* plastic lids, coffee can lids or similar 4" to 6" rubbery plastic lids, or carpet scraps, 6" squares, with flexible backing, like 'indoor-outdoor' carpet. A friendly carpet store should give you scraps or a parent can cut them with a mat knife.

C. Lay out the pieces in this pattern, on a solid driveway or garage floor if possible.

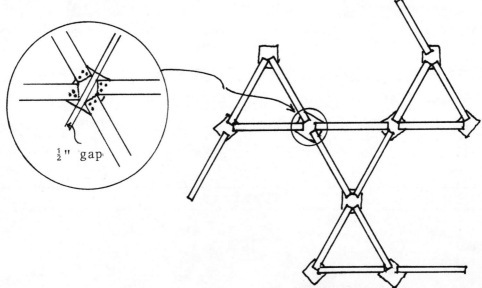

½" gap

D. Attach the hubs with ⅝" carpet tacks. Start with the center triangle. Leave ½" gap between the ends of the boards where the carpet will bend.

If you're not working on a solid surface, put a scrap of 2x4 under each hub as you nail it.

About the Flat Top

Buckminster Fuller would not have stopped with a flat top. It will catch rain. This design stops with the flat top because the next steps in dome building become complicated. Study your model. You may discover a solution. Or put a small hole in the center of the top so that rain won't tear the plastic. Sleep out on clear nights, not rainy ones.

THE SKIN

E. Find two friends to help you.

F. While the frame is still flat, unfold the 8 by 12 sheet of plastic over it.

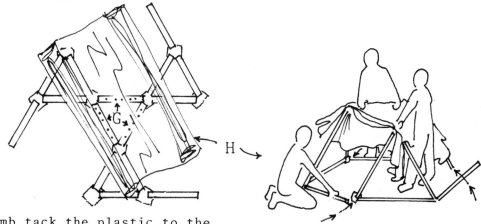

G. Thumb tack the plastic to the center triangle.

H. Fold the plastic back and out of your way. With your friends, lift the center and pull the 3 baseboards in place.

I. Attach the hubs to these boards with carpet tacks. Put the 2x4 behind the board to hold it for hammering.

J. Pull the plastic tight to the frame. Tuck it in; thumb tack it to the frame. Trim off extra.

Move your dome to a nice shady place and invite your friends in.

  Caution:
Plastic burns. Don't build campfires close to this tent.

83

ARCHIMEDES' SCREW

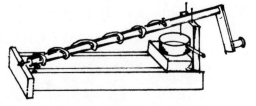

Archimedes lived more than 2100 years
ago in a colony of the Greek Empire.
He was the greatest of the ancient
mathematicians. You may have heard
the legend of one of his discoveries.

King Hieron of Syracuse posed this problem: Is my crown pure gold or
has silver been mixed with the gold? How can I tell? Archimedes puz-
zled over this as he prepared to bathe. He stepped into a full tub.
Water overflowed. He realized he could drop the crown into a full tub
of water, measure the overflow, and with that, calculate the purity
of the gold.

Put crown in
full tub. Catch
overflow.

water   gold

Make a pure
gold brick
*the same
volume as the
spilled water*.

Put gold brick and crown on a scale.

If they *balance*, the
crown weighs the same
as the brick and so
is pure gold.

If they *don't
balance*, the
crown weighs
less and so has
a lighter metal
(silver) in it.

Archimedes was so excited, he ran naked in the street shouting
'εὕρηκα,' meaning 'I have found it!' His word, 'Eureka,' has come
into our language as the word to celebrate the moment of discovery.

Archimedes' Water Screw, Κοχλίας in Greek, was the first machine
to replace the bucket-on-a-rope method of lifting water. He invented it to draw water from leaking boats. Farmers used it to
pump water to irrigate their crops. Later, Dutch windmills
powered it to drain lowlands. Its basic screw principle moves
grain and coal in modern machines.

The Water Screw remains mysterious. How does the water climb?
Your water screw will take patience and some adjustments. Experiment with it in the bathtub, and when you've got it working, you can join the ancient inventor with his word, EUREKA!

Materials		
2 ft.	tubing	see note next page
2 ft.	broomstick	1 in. diameter or larger: larger is better
4 ft.	1x3	
	can	cat food, tuna fish size
	plastic straw	
1	screweye	
	wood scraps	see 'The Crank' section
	glue	
	nails	4d, 8d, 1 in. brads
	rubberband	

Adjust the Project to Your Materials

The tubing is the heart of this project. Rubber tubing (from a drugstore or old shower sprayer), plastic tubing (from a hardware or plumbing store) or a scrap of garden hose will work. Each will bend differently. Look for tubing that will bend easily without going flat.

* Take your axle along to test tubing.
* Clear tubing lets you watch the water climb.
* $\frac{3}{8}$ in. inside diameter (I.D.) tubing usually works well.
* The tubing you use will set all the measurements for the project.
* You can make a giant screw or a tiny one.

The Coil

Try out the tubing and axle before you make any cuts. Soak the tubing in hot water to make it more flexible. Get some help.

Start 1 in. from the end. Make a coil of 5 or 6 turns (more if you wish). No coil will be perfectly smooth but thats ok if water can get through. When you get 6 in. from the top of the broomstick, uncoil the tubing and cut off what you don't need.

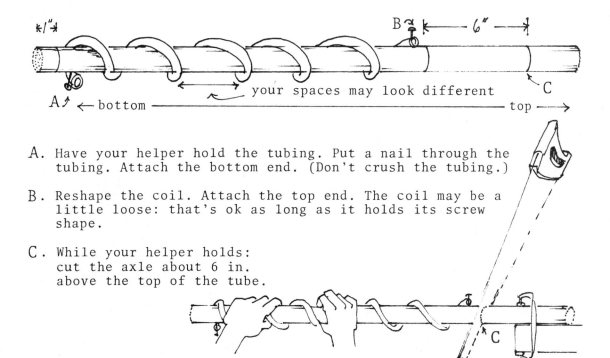

B ⟵ — 6" — ⟶

⟵ bottom ——————————————————————— top ⟶

your spaces may look different

A. Have your helper hold the tubing. Put a nail through the tubing. Attach the bottom end. (Don't crush the tubing.)

B. Reshape the coil. Attach the top end. The coil may be a little loose: that's ok as long as it holds its screw shape.

C. While your helper holds:
cut the axle about 6 in.
above the top of the tube.

The Frame

The frame's 4 pieces are all 1x3.

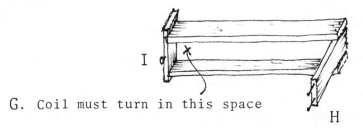

down
down
down

E

F

G   D

D. Cut the base pieces: about the same length the tubing covers on the axle.

E. Cut an upright piece. You have to estimate. The coils must always appear to tip down. From $\frac{1}{2}$ to $\frac{5}{8}$ the length of the base is a safe guess.

F. Nail (4d) the base pieces to the edges of the upright.

G. Nail a short piece of 1x3 across the end of the base. (Check your coil first. If it won't turn freely, use this end piece to spread the base.

I

G. Coil must turn in this space

H

H. Start 2 nails (8d) in the top of the upright to hold axle.

I. Put a screw eye in the middle of the end piece.

The Crank

Make a crank and handle from scraps. Simple cranks:

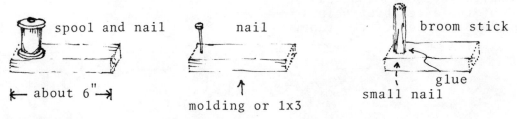

spool and nail   nail   broom stick

←— about 6" —→   glue

molding or 1x3   small nail

Work out your own design.

Reservoir

This catches the water you lift and carries it off.
Make one from a can and a plastic straw or design your own.

J. Punch a hole in the can near the rim.
To do this, make a support for the can's
side; start with a 4d nail, then go to
a bigger nail.

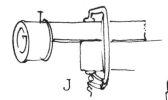

Twist and wiggle a pencil in the hole to open it just enough
to hold the straw. (This is called reaming.)

K. Seal the straw with a few drops of plastic cement.

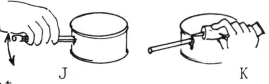

Experiment

L. Glue and nail the crank to the top end of the axle.

M. Support the crank on the edge of your bench.
Start a finishing nail in the center of the bottom.

N. Connect the reservoir with a rubber band.
Put a block for it to sit on.

NOW, slip the axle into the frame.
Place the frame in 2 or 3 inches of water.
Do you know which direction to crank?

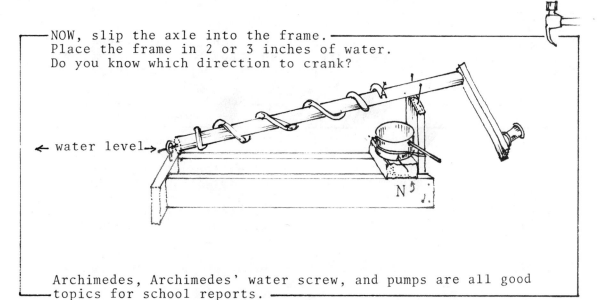

← water level →

Archimedes, Archimedes' water screw, and pumps are all good
topics for school reports.

SAVONIOUS' ROTOR

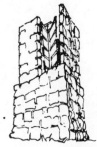

Inventors have created machines to put wind power to work on land for 1000 years--sails have moved ships for much longer. The first windmills, for grinding grain, were built in Persia.

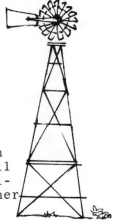

You've seen pictures of the great wooden mills that began draining the lowlands of Holland in the Middle Ages.

You may have seen a 'pinwheel' water pumper still standing on a farm. Daniel Halliday designed this wind catcher in 1854.

In the early 1900's, cheap electricity came to farms and factories. Wind machines were left to rust away. Since electricity is no longer cheap, scientists and engineers are again turning to the winds. A new age of wind power is beginning.

Some modern wind machines look like huge airplane propellers--and airplane science has shaped them. Others look like egg beaters.

S.J. Savonious created this S-shaped Rotor 50 years ago. It's not a completely new idea. Like the first Persian wind mill, it turns on a vertical axis.

The Rotor is a 'panamone'--an 'all wind' machine. Unlike the Dutch mill or Halliday's machine--it does not have to be aimed to face the wind. This simplicity makes it a popular machine for beginning experimentors.

Materials . . .for a Basic Rotor		
1	2-liter plastic soda bottle	look for one with straight sides
approx.12"	molding or broomstick	axle: the lighter the better
approx.16"	1x3 or 1x2	or other wood scraps
4'	1x3 or 1x2	for tower: any length will do
1	push pin	
2	screw eyes	
	nails	4d
	tacks	

THE ROTOR

Make the vanes

A. With pointed scissors, poke a hole to start. Cut the top and bottom from the plastic bottle.

B. Cut the cylinder into 2 equal halves.

C. Cut an axle about 2 inches longer than the vanes.

D. Tack the vanes to the axle.

E. Mark the center of the top and bottom of the axle. Put a push pin in one end. Start a nail in the other.

THE TOWER

F. Use the rotor to judge how long the crosspieces must be. Cut 2.

G. Put a screw eye in the end of each crosspiece.

H. Again using the rotor to measure, nail (4d) the crosspieces in place.

ASSEMBLY

I. The crosspieces will 'give' enough so that you can slip the rotor in place.

J. Make adjustments. Nothing should rub. Trim the vanes with scissors to balance them.

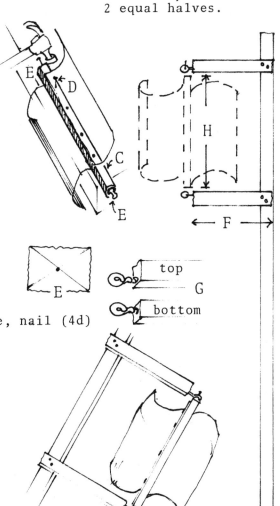

K. Experiment with the push pin end. Add a drop of oil or a washer to reduce friction.

GO FIND THE WIND!

EXPERIMENT

※Use your Rotor to test wind strength.

Where are the strongest winds in your neighborhood? What makes a place windy?

Attach a streamer (a piece of plastic) to the top of your Tower. Do the strongest winds come from one particular direction? Why?

※Build and test variations of the Rotor.

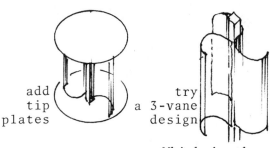

add tip plates   try a 3-vane design   try blocking wind on the back vane   try a 2-rotor axle

Which is the most powerful?

※Design your own wind machine. Name it after yourself.

ON YOUR OWN

If you live in a windy area, you could build a Savonious Rotor big enough to generate a tiny bit of electricity. You might start with a 5-gallon plastic bucket (a sheetrock compound bucket or a wax bucket from your school janitor,) roller skate wheels for bearings, and rubber tubing for power take-off.

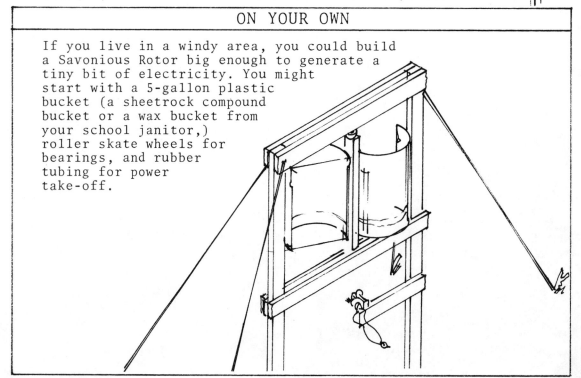

HAMMER MILL

You know what wheat looks like and flour, in your kitchen, but do you know how the kernels of wheat become flour?

If you had lived on a farm in 1700, you'd know. Grinding grain into flour would have been one of your regular chores. You might have ground the grain in a hollowed log, *mortar*, with a heavy wooden *pestle*, ancient tools. It was hard, slow work.

Hard work makes people inventive. You might have set about building the simplest of water machines, a plumping mill, to help.

Water flows into the box:
    the hammer rises.
Water spills out:
    the hammer falls 'plump.'

It's an ancient machine that may have appeared first in China. The Japanese built the bamboo *kakehi*, a little larger than the Hammer Mill you'll build, in temple gardens. Its work, legends say, was to scare away wild boars. It's trickling water and gentle 'klonks' became music in the quiet of the garden.

筧
— *kakehi*

A few plumping mills still grind grain. Modern grain, factory-ground at high speeds, cannot match its taste.

Materials		
about 4'	1x3	
12"	2x3 or 2x4	
6"	¼" dowel	or a pencil
1	orange juice can	cardboard or plastic, 16 oz. size
3"	broomstick	or a rock
1	cat food can	or similar size can
	rubber bands	
	nails	4d, tacks
	paint	

Stay loose. . .

The balance and angles of the mill are hard to guess. This project is designed to keep the pieces adjustable while you test the mill.

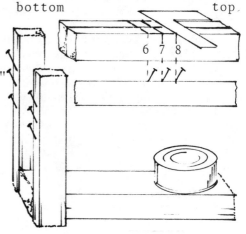

THE FRAME

A. Cut 2 1x3's, 12" long.

B. With your square, draw lines 6",7",8" from the bottom of both.

C. Start 4d nails on these lines. Tilt them toward the top.

D. Nail (4d) the uprights to a 12" long 2x3 or 2x4 base.

E. Attach a cat food can with a rubber band between 2 nails.

Some cans have bottoms like the bowl of a mortar for holding grain.

THE BEAM

F. With scissors, cut away half of one side of an orange juice can.

G. Start with a 16" long 1x3 beam: you may have to trim it later.

H. Start 2 (4d) nails into one end of the beam, to hold the hammer.

I. Connect the tip of a broom stick 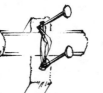 or a stone

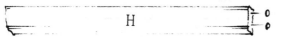

between the nails with rubber bands.

J. Connect the orange juice can and an axle ($\frac{1}{4}$" dowel or pencil) with rubber bands.

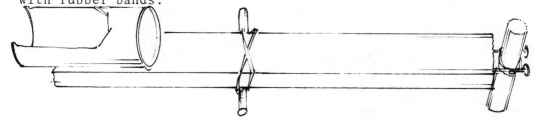

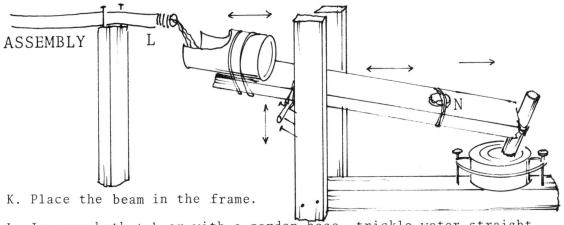

ASSEMBLY L

K. Place the beam in the frame.

L. In your bath tub or with a garden hose, trickle water straight
down into the can.

M. Adjust all the pieces until the beam rises and falls in a
steady rhythm.

N. A stone attached to the beam will give you one more adjustment if you need it.

O. When you're happy with the way it's working, you can staple
the axle in place and tack the orange juice can in place.

P. Let the beam dry over night and paint it: otherwise, it
will soak up water when it's operating and change its
balance.

ON YOUR OWN

The hammer is part of a mill. A mill needs a stream, a dam,
a pond and a *sluice way* to carry water to the hammer.

A *sluice gate* and *spill way* control the flow of water when
the pond floods.

Not every stream has a good mill site. Mill builders look for
sharp drops in a stream where a small dam will lift water
high enough to feed a mill.

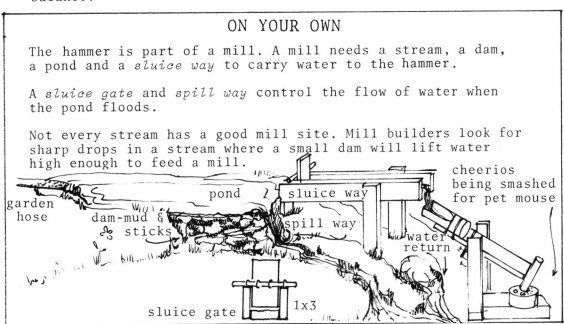

WATER WHEELS

Machines change the way people live. Sometimes the change is
so great that it's called a *revolution*. . . .Work, style of
living and even ways of thinking change. You know, for example,
that you and your friends will be part of the computer revolution that's just beginning.

The water wheel helped begin one of these revolutions. In
England, in the 1700's, the water wheel turned the first machines of the Industrial Revolution. The water wheel was not
a new machine. Its work was new. Its power poured into every
craft and labor. The first factories were organized on the banks
of English streams. Iron and cloth flowed from these factories.
Factories brought hard, dirty work, and prosperity.

It was an age of inventions put to work. The millwrights who
led the revolution had spent little time in schools: they were
craftsmen, not aristocrats. The mills were their classrooms.
Their art became the science of engineering.

By 1800, a new machine, the steam engine, brought even greater
power to the factories. It replaced the water wheel. But it was
the water wheel that had excited the dreamers and inventors
who set the revolution in motion.

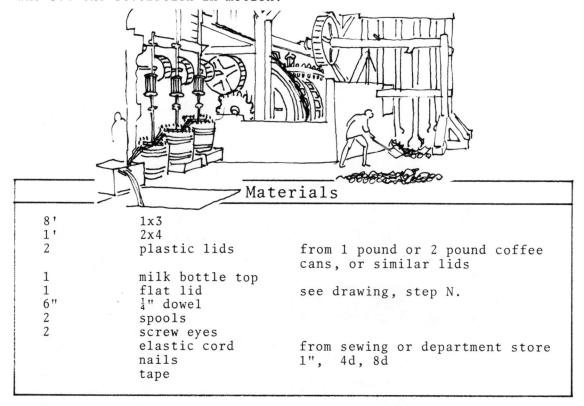

Materials

8'	1x3	
1'	2x4	
2	plastic lids	from 1 pound or 2 pound coffee cans, or similar lids
1	milk bottle top	
1	flat lid	see drawing, step N.
6"	$\frac{1}{4}$" dowel	
2	spools	
2	screw eyes	
	elastic cord	from sewing or department store
	nails	1", 4d, 8d
	tape	

WATER WHEEL TYPES

The water source, how much there is, how far it drops, how fast it flows, shapes the design of water wheels.

The water wheel in this project is designed to operate in a bath tub or under a garden hose.

A *flutter wheel* of this type would have been built under a swift water fall. ⟶

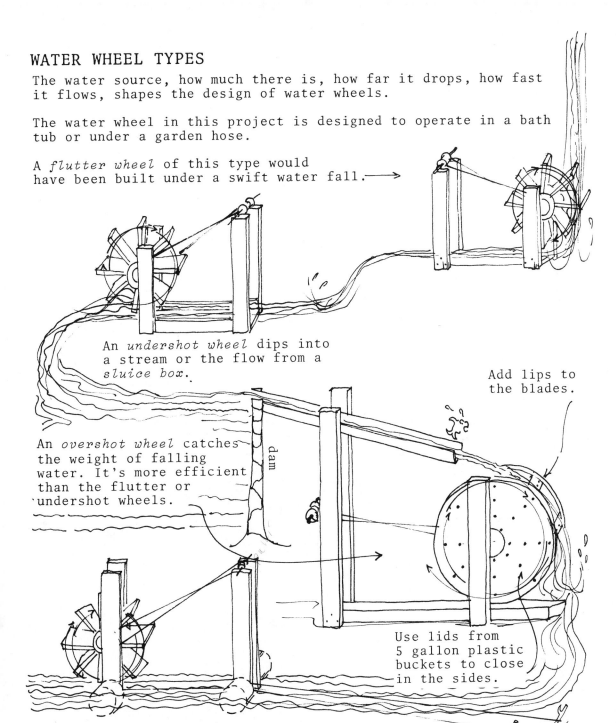

An *undershot wheel* dips into a stream or the flow from a *sluice box*.

Add lips to the blades.

An *overshot wheel* catches the weight of falling water. It's more efficient than the flutter or undershot wheels.

dam

Use lids from 5 gallon plastic buckets to close in the sides.

A *floating mill* is turned by the current of a river.   anchors

To make a floating mill, add coffee can *pontoons*. (See BOATS, Catamaran.)

THE WHEEL

Try this 10" flutter wheel first. When you've got the idea, experiment with other sizes and types.

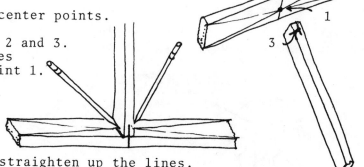

A. Cut 2 pieces of 1x3, 10" long.

B. Measure and mark 3 center points.

C. Match center points 2 and 3.
Draw along both sides
as far as center point 1.

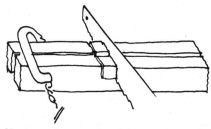

D. Use your square to straighten up the lines.
It should look like this:→

E. Clamp the 2 pieces together.
Cut both sides of the notch.

F. Hammer on this line.

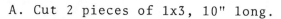

F. Use a large nail to break the
pieces out. (The nail is sub-
stituting for a chisel.)

G. Your 2 pieces shaped like this
will fit together to make the
edge lap joint that starts the
wheel.

You may have to trim the notches with your saw so they'll
fit. Or start over. *It's tricky!*

H. Cut 4 pieces of 1x3, 4½" long.
Lay the pieces out on your bench.
Recut any piece that doesn't fit
into the circle.

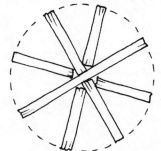

8 blades

I. Cut the rim or lip from a plastic coffee can lid.

J. Find the center of the lid. You'll feel a bump with your fingertip. Push a 1" nail through it.

K. Find the center of the wheel. Place the lid and nail (J) on that point. Tack it in *just a little*.

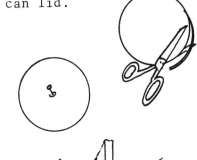

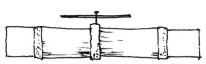

L. Have a friend hold the blades in place. Nail (1" nails) the lid to the cross pieces first, (go 1,2,3, then 4). Then nail in the other 4 blades.

M. Pull the center nail out. Turn wheel over. Repeat steps I,J,K,L, for the other side.

THE DRIVE PULLEY & AXLE

N. Drive an 8d nail through the center of a stiff, flat disk—an orange juice can top, a canning jar top—then through the center of a milk container top.

O. Then place that nail right on the center of a hub. Drive it in ½" or till it's firm.

P. Press the lids tight. Nail them into the wheel with 2 1" nails.

Q. Turn the wheel over. Sandwich the axle between 2 blocks.

R. Drive an 8d nail into the center of the hub.

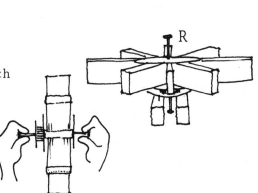

THE FRAME & DRIVING SHAFT

S. Cut 1 piece of 2x4 12" long. Try for careful, square cuts.
   Cut 4 pieces of 1x3, 12" long.

T. Mark lines across a pair of
   the 1x3's at 7 and 8 inches
   from the bottom.

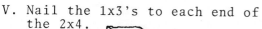

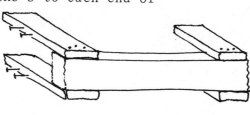

U. Start 4d nails on those lines,
   tilted toward the top.

V. Nail the 1x3's to each end of
   the 2x4.

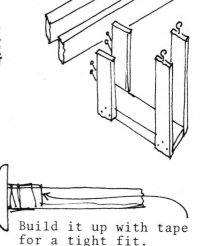

W. Start screw eyes in the tops
   of the back pair of supports.

X. Fit two spools on a 6" piece of $\frac{1}{4}$" dowel.

Build it up with tape
for a tight fit.

ASSEMBLY

Y. Work the driving shaft into the screw eyes.
   Rest the wheel on a pair of nails, with the drive pulley
   on the same side as the large spool.

Z. Connect the drive pulley to
   the driving shaft with a
   loop of elastic cord.

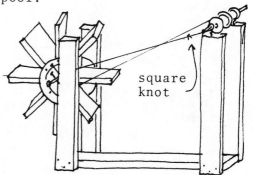

square
knot

MILLWORKS

Water teaches. The sea educated explorers. The water wheel
educated inventors.

Belts carry power from the water wheel to machines. The machines
turn, spin, grind, thump, push and pull. It's *visible* energy.
You can see it work; you can hear it; you can feel its vibrations.
It's an active teacher.

Millwrights watched men and women laboring. They asked, 'How
can I bring the power of my wheel to that task?' Their first
machines imitated those men and women at work, grinding, sawing,
hammering, pumping, lifting.

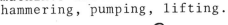

You can build these machines on your own. Learn as the millwrights
learned. Discover ways to step up your mill's power. Invent the
parts you need. Experiment until your machines work: until they
look right, sound right, feel right.

Then design your own machines:

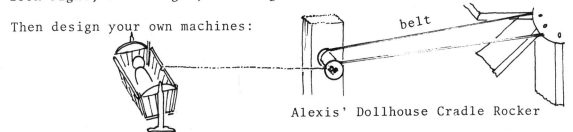

Alexis' Dollhouse Cradle Rocker

In 1760, English millwrights combined the movements of the basic
mill tools to perform complex tesks: to spin fibers into thread,
to weave thread into cloth. They believed their tools and common
sense and nature's power could lighten every labor. That confidence set in motion remarkable changes.

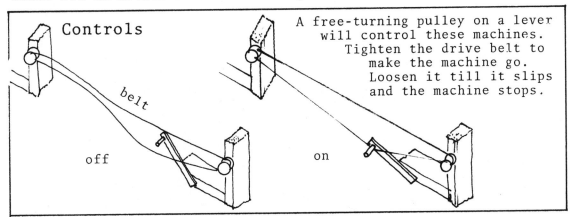

Controls

A free-turning pulley on a lever
will control these machines.
Tighten the drive belt to
make the machine go.
Loosen it till it slips
and the machine stops.

belt

off

on

PULLEYS. . .

transmit power. . .reverse it. . .

change power and speed. . .change direction

You'll need pulleys of different sizes. . .that you can connect to axles or to each other. Adapt your designs to what you can find or put together.

Look for Pulley Shapes. . .

Spools are easiest to use.

thread spool

bobbin

string or ribbon spool

tinkertoy

pulley from block or other machine

Build up axle with tape, so pulley will fit tight.

wheel from toy (rubber tire removed)

Or Make Pulleys. . .

Build up *rims* on a broomstick. . . . . .or put together lids

pipe cleaner

card board

some orange juice lids are shaped like half pulleys

rubber bands

cord with staple & glue

washers on a dowel

2 flat lids and a lid with straight sides

Getting to the Middle of it. . .

Trace around the lid. . .
Cut out the pattern. . .

Fold the pattern in half. . .in half again.

Open it: X markes the middle.

EXPERIMENTS
Start with experiments right on your water wheel.

Add a disk with bright colors. . .

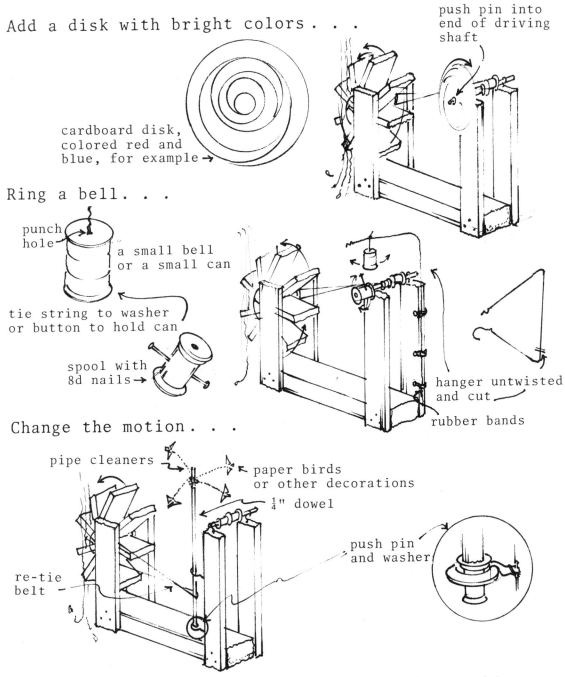

push pin into
end of driving
shaft

cardboard disk,
colored red and
blue, for example →

Ring a bell. . .

punch
hole

a small bell
or a small can

tie string to washer
or button to hold can

spool with
8d nails →

hanger untwisted
and cut

rubber bands

Change the motion. . .

pipe cleaners

paper birds
or other decorations

$\frac{1}{4}$" dowel

push pin
and washer

re-tie
belt

...and then try more complex machines...

On Your Own: A Plan for Finding Your Own Plan

1. Study the project.
   Draw it out.
   Ask yourself questions about it.

   Picture it in your mind.

2. Gather materials.
   Figure out which materials are important,
   and which you can substitute for.

   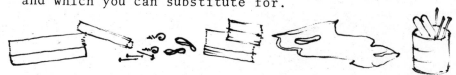

3. Start with a base. (A one foot long 2x4 will work for the water
   works projects.)

4. Before you cut or nail, hold
   together scraps (with your hands
   or rubber bands) to see how the
   project should fit together.

   Mark the scraps for cutting.

5. Ask yourself: What should be cut and attached *first?*
   Where should you leave room for adjustment?
   How can you leave room for adjustment?

   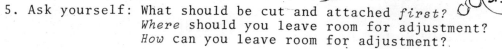

6. As you build, test your piece
   at each stage.

   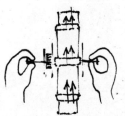

7. Remember: not many important inventions worked on their very
   first test. Make time for adjustments part of your plan.

   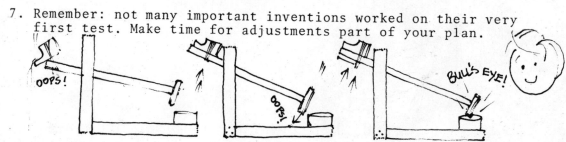

OOPS!   OOPS!   BULL'S EYE!

GRIST MILLS

In 180 B.C., the Roman architect, Vitruvius, discovered a grain mill of this type. The teeth of the gear sent the power up through a fixed stone to turn a top stone. The miller poured grain through the center of the top stone. Flour and bran dropped from the rim of the stones.

In 1840, there were over 20,000 small mills in America, many of them similar to this design. By the time your grandfather was your age, gasoline or electric powered mills had replaced all but a few of the water-powered mills.

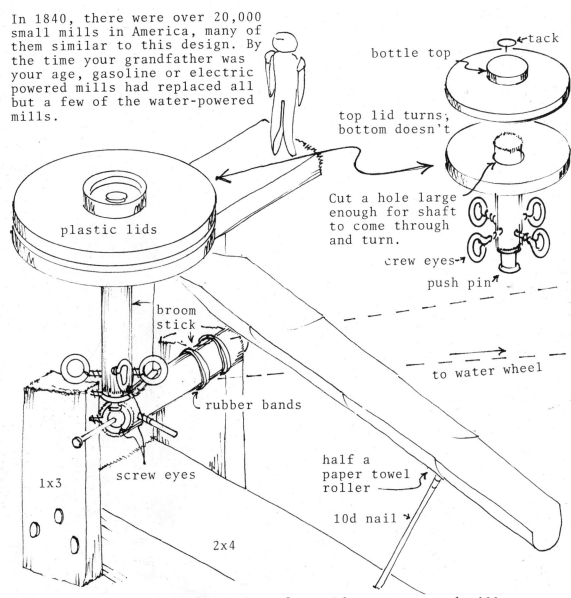

bottle top

tack

top lid turns, bottom doesn't

plastic lids

Cut a hole large enough for shaft to come through and turn.

crew eyes

push pin

broom stick

to water wheel

rubber bands

half a paper towel roller

1x3

screw eyes

10d nail

2x4

You may be able to find remains of an old water-powered mill near your home town.

SAW
Mills prepared wood for building.

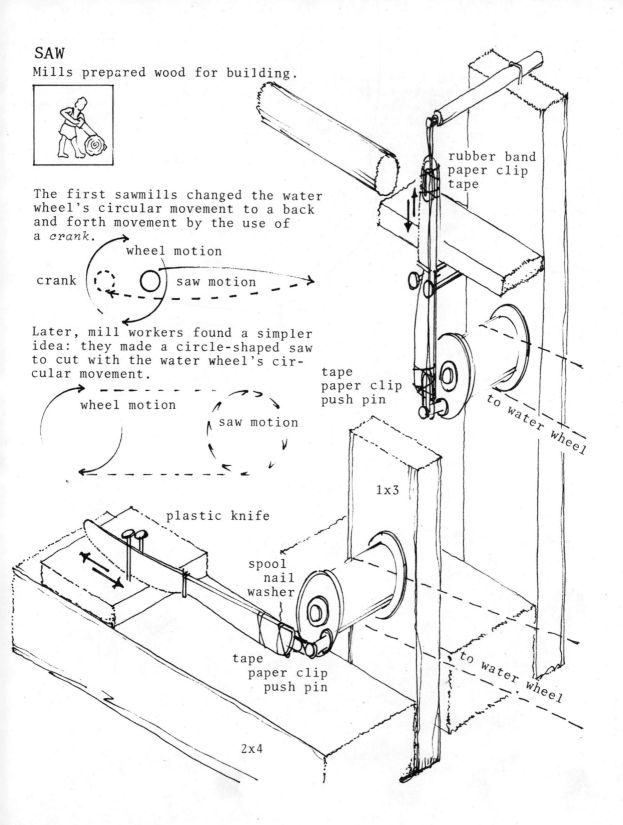

The first sawmills changed the water
wheel's circular movement to a back
and forth movement by the use of
a *crank*.

wheel motion

crank

saw motion

Later, mill workers found a simpler
idea: they made a circle-shaped saw
to cut with the water wheel's circular movement.

wheel motion

saw motion

rubber band
paper clip
tape

tape
paper clip
push pin

to water wheel

1x3

plastic knife

spool
nail
washer

tape
paper clip
push pin

to water wheel

2x4

BELLOWS & TRIP HAMMER

The bellows fanned the blacksmiths' fires, and the trip hammer shaped the red-hot iron. *Cams* set both in motion.

These were tools for making other tools. They forged the iron and steel that began to replace wood in the building of machines.

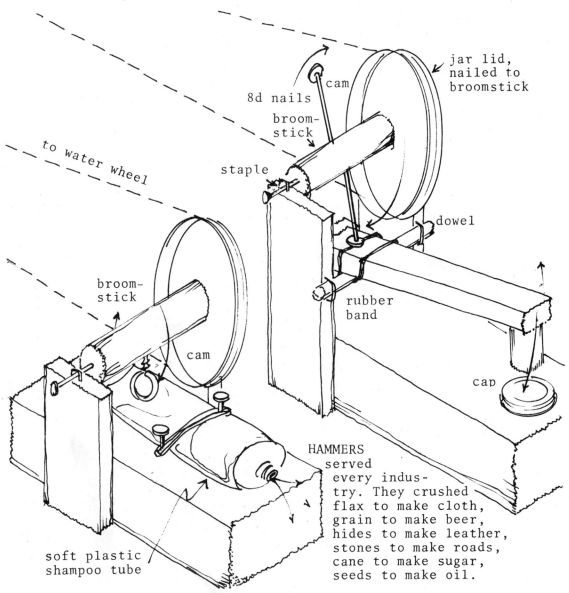

jar lid, nailed to broomstick

cam

8d nails

broom-stick

to water wheel

staple

dowel

broom-stick

cam

rubber band

cap

soft plastic shampoo tube

HAMMERS served every industry. They crushed flax to make cloth, grain to make beer, hides to make leather, stones to make roads, cane to make sugar, seeds to make oil.

PUMP

Pumps were crucial to the Industrial Revolution. They supplied water to the towns that grew up around factories. They drained water from coal mines. Modern cylindrical pumps, invented to make deep mines safe, replaced this ancient bucket pump.

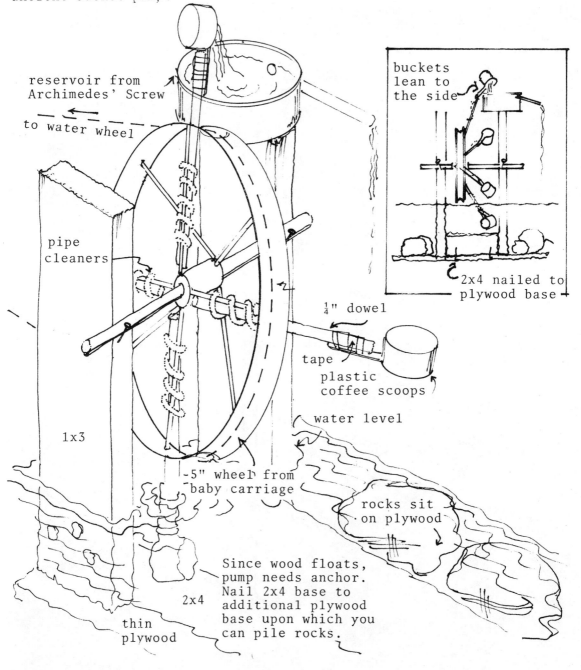

reservoir from Archimedes' Screw

to water wheel

pipe cleaners

buckets lean to the side

2x4 nailed to plywood base

$\frac{1}{4}$" dowel

tape
plastic coffee scoops

water level

1x3

5" wheel from baby carriage

rocks sit on plywood

Since wood floats, pump needs anchor. Nail 2x4 base to additional plywood base upon which you can pile rocks.

2x4

thin plywood

CRANE

Cranes were added to
mills to lift ore,
timber, grains and
other loads.

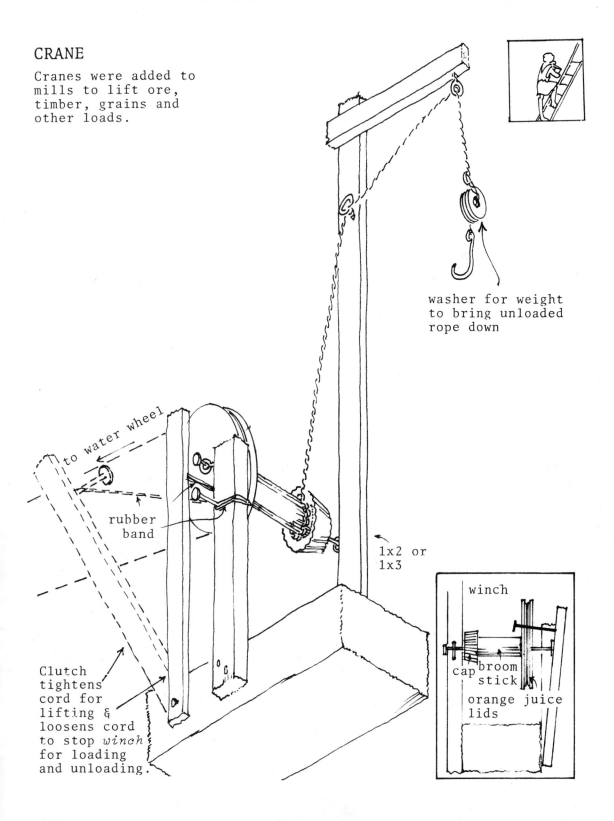

washer for weight
to bring unloaded
rope down

to water wheel

rubber
band

1x2 or
1x3

Clutch
tightens
cord for
lifting &
loosens cord
to stop *winch*
for loading
and unloading.

winch

cap

broom
stick

orange juice
lids

THE GENERATOR

Improved steam engines powered railroads.
Railroads carried coal to steam engines
in factories where there were not streams.
The water wheel might have been abandoned.

In 1860, the electric generator was invented. High speed turbines replaced the
water wheel. Generators replaced direct
drive mill machinery.

A new era of water power began.
And a new revolution began.

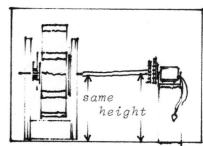

same height

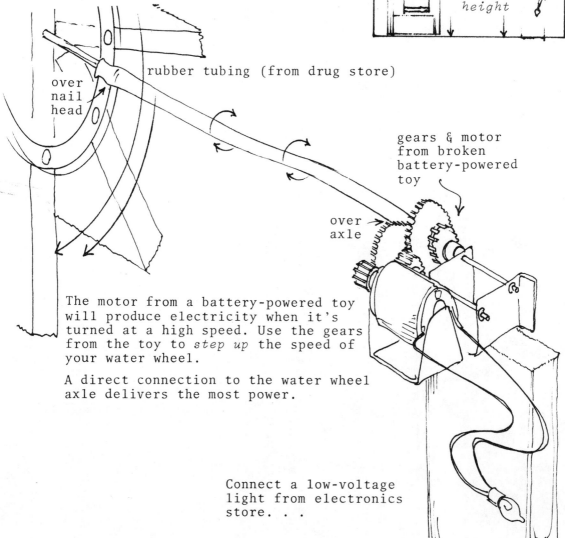

rubber tubing (from drug store)

over
nail
head

gears & motor
from broken
battery-powered
toy

over
axle

The motor from a battery-powered toy
will produce electricity when it's
turned at a high speed. Use the gears
from the toy to *step up* the speed of
your water wheel.

A direct connection to the water wheel
axle delivers the most power.

Connect a low-voltage
light from electronics
store. . .

APPENDIX
1: Knots

Knots are simple *after* you've learned them. Their usefulness
is clear *after* you've learned them. But learning knots from
the drawings flat on this page is tricky. The best approach is
to fiddle and fiddle with a piece of cord until you catch on to
each knot. Practice until you can tie each knot with your eyes
closed.

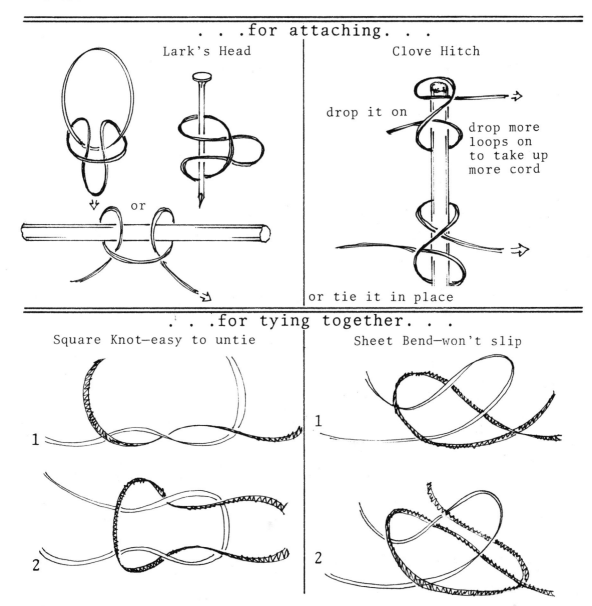

. . .for attaching. . .

Lark's Head   Clove Hitch

drop it on

drop more
loops on
to take up
more cord

or

or tie it in place

. . .for tying together. . .

Square Knot—easy to untie   Sheet Bend—won't slip

1   1

2   2

2: Tools of Choice

You will have to search to find tools just right for you. Stores may not always carry the sizes you need and manufacturers change and discontinue tools. The guidelines we've offered here should help your hardware dealer recommend similar tools if the specific tools we've named are not available.

If you can't find the tools you need, send us a self-addressed, stamped envelope for an updated list of the tools we recommend and distribute:

> Wood Works
> 206 Willow Street
> New Haven, CT   06511

Hammer

You'll see many hammers to choose from. Try out as many hammers as you can, before you buy one. Consider:

Weight: The weight of the hammer's head will be marked on
          its label: 7 oz., 8 oz., 13 oz., or 16 oz. Not all
          hammers of the same weight feel the same. Easco's
          7 oz. hammer, for example, is too light to work with.
          A hammer should feel *a little* heavy but not awkward.

Grip: We've recommended 7 and 8 oz. hammers because their
          handles fit a small hand comfortably. Choose a hammer
          with a handle your hand can wrap around firmly.

Safety: *Do not* buy a hammer with a *cast* head. These bargain
          hammers are dangerous. The label on your hammer should
          say *forged head*. The hammer's construction should be
          smooth and sturdy. In low priced hammers, wooden
          handles are just as strong as metal handles.

The three most popular hammers in our classes are,

Oxwall	1323	8 oz.	$4.75
Sears	3806	7 oz.	7.25
Stanley	213	7 oz.	7.00

Sears, Stanley, and other major manufacturers offer 16 oz. hammers that are less expensive than these 7 or 8 oz. hammers.

Saw

Finding a saw that will meet all your needs is difficult. Look at:

Teeth: Look for 7 to 10 teeth per inch: that number will be marked on the label. A saw with more than 10 teeth per inch will clog easily in the soft wood you will work with.

Length: *A short saw blade length*, 16 to 20 inches is ideal. Unfortunately, usually only very good (expensive) or very bad saws are sold in this length. You may have to settle for a 26-inch blade: that's a little longer and more awkward than you need.

Economy: You will be hard on your first saw. Beginners bend blades as they learn. Look for a moderately priced saw so that you can feel comfortable learning with it.

Choices:
A used saw: Look for an old saw with a straight blade that is not badly rusted. You might find one at a tag sale, you uncle's house, etc. *Have it sharpened.* Look under SAWS-Sharpening in the Yellow Pages. The cost is usually $3 or $4. Good choices are,

Stanley Hardtooth	#15 355	$ 7.00
Sandvik	#297.7T*	11.00
Sears	# 36136	9.00

Consumer Reports (May 1983) rates this saw as a 'Best Buy.'

Goggles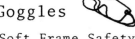

Soft Frame Safety Goggles are recommended for complete eye protection. Some people find goggles uncomfortable. Eye shields and glasses are mentioned here because you must find a type of eye protection you will use *every time you use tools.*

Soft Frame Safety Goggles:

Sears	# 1859	} $3.00
Stanley	54 060	

Eye Shields (clear plastic spectacles, lightweight):

Norton # JJ12 $2.00

Glasses

Some health plans and corporation safety programs will provide safety glasses at little or no cost.

Even ordinary prescription glasses have tempered lenses which provide considerable eye protection.

Clamps

Look for:

Opening: at least 4 inches

Weight: Light or medium weight clamps can be well made. Avoid
         flimsy clamps: they work poorly and break fast.

4" C-clamps: Department stores with hardware sections often
         carry light weight C-clamps. For example,

                Brinks & Cotton #114 $4.00

6" Bar Clamps: more flexible, but slightly more expensive and
         difficult to find.

                Jorgensen   #3706 $7.00

Tag Sales and flea markets are a good source for clamps.

Squares

Squares are either very expensive or very cheap. You don't need an
expensive square. Look for:

A Stamped Metal Try Square: Unfortunately, few hardware stores
carry these. Often you find them at flea markets.

Combination Square: These are available (Sears 39555,) but are
not ideal because they slide apart: the parts are easily lost.

Plastic & Metal Try Square: Stanley   46.502 $4.50
                               Royal Tools #815   2.00

A Plastic T-Square: Although not a wood worker's square, a
plastic t-square will meet your needs and is easy to find in
any store with a large school supply section.

                Sterling   #542 $1.00

Measurer

Measuring tapes are expensive ($6 or more) and very easy to break.

A plastic or wooden ruler is always reliable. 16" or 18" is a use-
ful length, but an ordinary 1' ruler will measure anything you want
it to. Look for rulers in school supply stores.

3: Shopping List

These materials will equip you to build most of the projects in
this book. The Glider, Sail, the Flag Pole, and the Tent are projects that will require a special shopping trip when you are ready
for them. Prices are shown for general reference. They vary wide-
ly from store to store and with different packaging.

	1x3	2x3	2x4	Plywood	Dowel
Practice				$2^{+}-\frac{3}{4}$"	
Thaumatrope	1'				
Pinball Machine				3 $-\frac{3}{4}$"	
Easy Glider	3'		4'		
Wooden Relatives	2'				
Boats	2'		1'	2 $-\frac{1}{4}$"	12 $-\frac{1}{4}$"
Wind Car	1'				36 $-\frac{1}{4}$"
					72 $-\frac{1}{2}$"
Mousetrap Tractor	1'				10 $-\frac{1}{4}$"
Archimedes Screw	4'				6 $-\frac{1}{4}$"
Savonious Rotor	6'				
Hammer Mill	4'		1'		6 $-\frac{1}{4}$"
Water Wheel	8'		1'		6 $-\frac{1}{4}$"
Mill Works	8'		3'		12 $-\frac{1}{4}$"
	40'	4'	6'	5 $-\frac{3}{4}$"	3-36 $-\frac{1}{4}$"
				3 $-\frac{1}{4}$"	2-36 $-\frac{1}{2}$"

$^{+}$sq. ft.

WOOD

5	8 foot pieces*....1x3 firring.........	$.50-.70,	each piece
1	4 foot piece.....2x3...............	** .14-.20,	per foot
6	1 foot pieces.....2x4...............	** .16-.25,	per foot
5	12" x12", aprox... $\frac{1}{2}$"-$\frac{3}{4}$" plywood.....	** .20-.70,	per sq. ft.
3	12" x12", aprox... $\frac{1}{4}$"or 4mm plywood..	** .20-.30,	per sq. ft.
3	36" .... $\frac{1}{4}$" dowels..........	.16-.22,	each
2	36" .... $\frac{1}{8}$" dowels.........	.14-.20,	each
	36" (for boats)···1x3 or 1x4 pine...	** .24-.36,	per foot
	64" (for boats)···stop molding.......	.15-.20,	per foot

*Cut these in half, if you wish, for easy transportation and storage.

**Try to find, rather than buy, these. They're common scraps.
  They're easiest to use already cut up.

HARDWARE

```
1 box..........1" nails, 16 or 17 gauge.....$ .60- .70, per box
1 pound........4d nails......................  .60-1.00, per pound
1 pound........8d nails......................  .60-1.00, per pound
1 box..........⅝" carpet tacks...............  .60- .75, per box
1 box..........½" staples....................  .60- .75, per box
10............W14 or W112 Screw eyes........  .06- .08. each
4 oz. bottle...white glue....................  .90-1.10
1 oz. tube.....all-purpose cement............1.70-2.00
1 roll........plastic electrical tape.......  .80-1.30
1 pack........assorted rubber bands.........  .40- .50
```

MISCELLANEOUS

Small nails and tacks
are sold in 2 or 3 ounce boxes.

Materials to be found or purchased as needed.

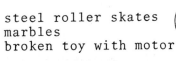

log for practice nailing

push pins
thumbtacks
paper clips
washers

broomsticks
wooden clothespins   people shaped
toothpicks
spools
tongue depressors

pipe cleaners
string   assorted types
rubber tubing
plastic tubing
mousetrap

steel roller skates
marbles
broken toy with motor

plastic spoons
plastic straws
garbage bags
plastic shopping bags
plastic lids from coffee cans
bottle caps

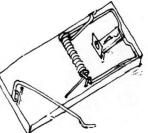

4: Benches

Benches need the planning and skills of an adult. Here are two simple and inexpensive designs. If the work looks difficult for you, have a friend with a power saw cut the pieces to size: the' rest will follow easily.

BOX TOP . . . . .

Materials

1	wood or plastic milk or soda case	sizes vary: 13"x13" to 13"x24" approx $4-6 if you buy
approx 6'	2x3	approx $1
approx 18"x24"	¾" plywood	Do-it-Yourself Stores sell pieces about this size approx $2
glue nails	6d finishing	

General Plan: Build the top around the box, for a tight fit. Trim the plywood and 2x3's after they're put together.

A. Cut the 2x3 into: 2 pieces 3" longer than the box's length, 2 pieces 3" longer than the box's width.

B. Start with the plywood, good side down. Put the box on it.

C. Apply glue to a face of each 2x3 and arrange in this pattern.

D. Start along the edges of a square corner. Fasten the first and second 2x3's with 2 nails each.

E. Press the third and fourth 2x3's against the box while you fasten them, also with two nails.

F. Take the lid off the box. Rest it on a solid surface. Put 4 more nails through the top into each of the 2x3's.

G. Trim off the extra plywood and 2x3.

H. Sand off the rough edges.

I. Bricks or a sand bag give this bench extra stability.

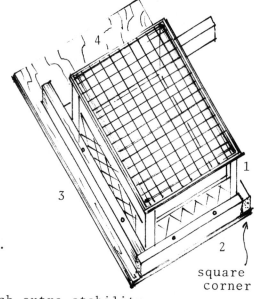

square corner

SAW HORSE . . .

Materials

1 pr	saw horse brackets	wood or plastic
		approx $2-7
10'	2x4	approx $2
4'	1x3	approx $ .50
8" x24"	¾" plywood	approx $2
	nails	6d finishing
		10d common
	glue	

General Plan: Make a sawhorse following the instructions for the brackets you buy, with a plywood top added for more work area.

TOP

A. Cut the plywood for the top to size.

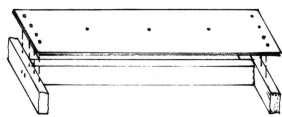

B. Cut 2 pieces of 2x4 as long as the width of the top.
   Cut 1 piece of 2x4 as long as the length of the top *minus 3"*.

C. Drill 2 pilot holes through the end pieces, to avoid splitting.

D. Glue and nail those end pieces to the center support.

E. Glue and nail the plywood top to that frame.

LEGS

F. Cut 4 legs: 18" for people under 5' tall,
   20" for people 5' tall and taller.

The brackets may have a guide for cutting the angle for the bottom of the leg. Otherwise, cut the legs an extra inch long, assemble the sawhorse, mark the angle and trim.

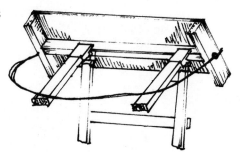

G. Attach the legs according to the instructions on the brackets.

H. Brace at least one pair of legs with 1x3: glue and nail.

I. A strap or rope will make the bench easy to carry.